JIGGLE!

Peter DiMario
Judith Choate

JIGGLE!
A Cookbook

50 Recipes for Sweet, Savory, and Sometimes Boozy Modern Gelatins

WORKMAN PUBLISHING
NEW YORK

Workman
Workman Publishing
Hachette Book Group, Inc.
1290 Avenue of the Americas
New York, NY 10104
workman.com

Workman is an imprint of Workman Publishing, a division of Hachette Book Group, Inc. The Workman name and logo are registered trademarks of Hachette Book Group, Inc.

Design by Becky Terhune
Cover photo by Eric Medsker

Library of Congress Cataloging-in-Publication Data
Names: DiMario, Peter, author. | Choate, Judith, author.
Title: Jiggle! : a cookbook : 50 recipes for sweet, savory, and sometimes boozy modern gelatins / Peter DiMario, Judith Choate.
Description: First edition. | New York, NY : Workman Publishing, [2024] | Includes index.
Identifiers: LCCN 2024012665 | ISBN 9781523525522 (hardcover) | ISBN 9781523525522 (epub)
Subjects: LCSH: Cooking (Gelatin) | LCGFT: Cookbooks.
Classification: LCC TX814.5.G4 D56 2024 | DDC 641.86/4—dc23/eng/20240327
LC record available at https://lccn.loc.gov/2024012665

First Edition October 2024
Printed in China on responsibly sourced paper.

10 9 8 7 6 5 4 3 2 1

**For Mom, who taught me
that everything tastes sweeter
when made with love.**

Contents

Preface

How I Learned to Love Gelatin

I love the magic of the theater. The thrill of the lights, colors, and sounds enthralls me. I play with these elements daily in my work as a documentary filmmaker, so it makes perfect sense that my culinary adventures would focus on the unlimited colors and shapes offered when working with gelatin. Like most Americans, I grew up with a frequent snack or dessert of shimmery, fruity JELL-O. But I lost interest in the jiggly stuff over the years, and by the time I reached adulthood, it had basically been relegated to memories of cafeteria lunches and occasional school sick days. It wasn't until I had free time during the COVID-19 lockdown that I rediscovered the food's wiggly pleasures. I began playing with the unusual flavors and shades I invented using unflavored gelatin, fruits, natural juices, and my imagination, and I realized that I could devise creations that were as exciting as a theatrical production.

During the height of the COVID-19 pandemic when—for better or worse—I had almost unlimited time to focus on translating my ideas into reality, the magic was intoxicating. I searched the internet for unusual molds, exciting food-safe dyes, and dazzling decor. It was alchemy as I turned plain sheets of gelatin into sparkling, colorful extravaganzas that still jiggled and wiggled just like that childhood bowl of JELL-O. I will admit to a fair share of #jellofails, but when I got it right, the results were awe-inspiring showstoppers. And I learned that although the extravagant results looked complicated to do, they were easily accomplished with time and patience.

I became fascinated with the art of deconstructing standard flavor profiles and turning them inside out. I turned some of my favorite classic desserts, drinks, and even savory dishes into jiggly and often sparkling multilayered confections. My kitchen started to feel like an artist's studio as I molded (pardon the pun) my ideas into gelatin form.

I spent almost two years in my gelatin lab. And once friends and family were able to safely gather, my creations moved from experiments to a much-welcomed signature addition to every party. I do hope that I have translated the fun I have had into an alluring adventure for you, the reader. You won't believe how creative you can get while experimenting with something so simple and easy to do!

JiGGLE!

Introduction

Tips and Tools

In the 1950s, gelatin took off. As part of molded salads, fruit gelatin, and aspic dishes, it appeared in a wide variety of colors and flavors. Over time, culinary creativity has expanded the use of gelatin, incorporating it through a broader spectrum of applications. Today, gelatin can take form in anything from intricate molecular gastronomy techniques in fine dining to the production of gummy candies, panna cotta, and even soups and stews. Plant-based alternatives that don't compromise on efficacy or flavor are also more readily available. Don't skip this section before setting off on your jelling journey. Executing these recipes, which may seem complicated, is easy with the right know-how. So, I've broken down everything you need to know. Learn a bit about your jelling options and molds, and discover the best ways to make sure your creations come out right.

Jelling Agents

Although there are a few products that can be used for jelling, in this book I focus on the two that are readily available and produce the best results: gelatin and agar agar. Gelatin can be purchased in sheets or as powder in small packets. Agar agar is sold as both powder and flakes or in strips.

GELATIN

Unlike packaged dessert gelatins, such as JELL-O, unflavored gelatin is totally flavorless and sugar-free. It has very few calories and can be used in sweet or savory dishes as well as in drinks. There are two types of unflavored gelatin readily available to the home cook. *Sheet gelatin* (also called leaf gelatin) produces crystal-clear results as well as a set jelly that is odorless, holds its shape, and shimmies beautifully. It melts just below body temperature, so it gently dissolves on your tongue as you embrace the flavor. Sheets are available online or from cake and baking supply stores. When a finished product requires clarity and translucence, I always use sheet gelatin.

Powdered gelatin is the form I use when definition and clarity are not essential. Although there are a variety of powders available, most supermarkets carry Knox Unflavored Gelatine, and that's my preference for its accessibility and reliability. It comes in 7-gram (about 2½-teaspoon) packets, each of which will set 2 cups (473 ml) of liquid.

Both the sheets and powder are made up of collagen proteins extracted from animal by-products—generally from pigskin, but also from cow's skin, bone, or horn. When using gelatin, it is important that you use the proper amount; too little and it won't set, too much and the finished gel will be rubbery and unpleasant in the mouth. I learned this well as I experimented and created new recipes. It's not very appetizing to have a finished dish that melts on the plate or bounces like a ball!

AGAR AGAR

This is a seaweed-derived thickener available as a powder or in flakes or strips. Because it is plant-based, it is commonly used to make vegan jams, jellies, puddings, custards, and other jellied recipes. It is extremely popular throughout Asia in confectionery and many types of desserts. Generally, a smaller amount of agar agar is required to set a product. Agar agar flakes require 1 tablespoon per cup of liquid while the powder uses only 1 teaspoon per cup of liquid. Once combined, however, it must be reheated to over 185°F (85°C) for about 7 minutes to melt. Highly acidic ingredients will often require experimentation to realize the correct amount of agar

Picking the Right Grade

Sheet gelatin is often found in a range of grades ascending, for example, from bronze grade to platinum grade—the higher the grade, the more clear your gelatin will be. For any recipe where you want perfectly clear, crystalline gelatin, use platinum grade. Experiment and see which works best for you!

Where It All Began

The role of gelatin in the culinary world goes back centuries, when savory concoctions were at the center of the tables of the rich and royal. The gelatin itself was originally made from animal collagen, which came from boiling hoofed animal's feet, bones, and horns in vast amounts of water, skimming off the impurities as they cooked, and clarifying the liquid with copious amounts of egg whites until it formed a fairly clear but very meaty-tasting broth. When left to set, the broth would be gelatinous. Because of its meaty flavor, the gelatin was generally used to make molded entrées, pastry-encased pies, and other meat-based recipes. Through time, just pig's feet or isinglass (from a fish's dried swim bladder) was used to make the collagen-rich broth necessary to gel a recipe, and because the latter was less meaty in flavor, it was used to create sweets as well.

agar that will be required to make a firm mold. I dislike using agar agar in my jiggles; recipes made with it lack the clarity and clean mouthfeel of those made with sheet or powdered gelatin. Its stability also makes it very difficult to unmold. That's why I call nearly exclusively for gelatin throughout the recipes in this book (and encourage you to follow suit!).

OTHER GELLING AGENTS

The other two jelling agents are *gellan gum* and *carrageenan*, which are used for commercial purposes and are not available to the home cook. The former is most frequently used as a commercial stabilizer or binder in candy, preserves, and plant-based "milk" products. Carrageenan, a plant-based jelling agent (derived from Irish moss, a red seaweed found along the Atlantic coast of the British Isles, continental Europe, and North America), has been used to stabilize, thicken, and gel food products for generations. Today, it is often used as a stabilizer in many commercially produced vegan products.

Foolproof Jiggles

Follow these tips to achieve perfect results using any type of gelatin.

- Acids, particularly those from citrus juices, can inhibit proper jelling and are generally not used when making gelatins.

- Some fresh fruits, such as pineapple, papaya, guava, figs, mango, pawpaw, and kiwi (as well as raw gingerroot), have a high content of protein-digesting enzymes that will inhibit the jelling process. These sorts of fruits—and their juices—need to be cooked (or pasteurized in the case of juice) to allow proper jelling.
- When adding fruit to gelatin dishes, take care that it is dry because excess juice will thin the gelatin mixture and affect the finished result. Canned fruit is usually quite juicy so it should be patted very dry before adding.
- When you want to suspend fruit or other solid ingredients within a layer of gelatin, you must first allow the gelatin to partially set (this usually takes at least 15 minutes in the refrigerator). At this point, you can fold in the solids, then refrigerate further until the mixture is set completely (typically about 1 hour, but each recipe will list the proper time). It's important to let one layer set before adding another layer of gelatin or other ingredients to the mold.
- When adding fruit to gelatin, particularly clear gelatin, take care that the pieces are neatly cut to bite-size. This is as much for aesthetic reasons as for ease of eating. You don't want large hunks of fruit marring the design of your gelatin dish.
- High-proof alcohol (above 40%) in high quantities will prevent jelling, so don't go over the suggested amount listed in the ingredient list.
- The longer a jelled product is refrigerated, the sturdier it will be. But any longer than 24 hours and it will get too dry, so, as a general rule, make your mold max 24 hours before your event.
- Any jelled product that is milk-based will set to a very firm texture.
- You can use any type of sweetener—natural or artificial—depending upon your needs.

A Word About Molds

Most of us are familiar with those sparkling copper molds that decorate many a kitchen wall. Some molds are just that—decorative rather than made for practical use. However, there are a great many beautiful antique or modern copper molds that are made specifically for gelatin presentations. Copper is an amazing conductor of heat. When the bottom of a copper mold is immersed in warm water, the metal's quick heat conduction allows the surface of the gelatin to warm just enough that

Molds Worthy of a King

At the height of Victorian culinary excesses, jellied dishes were much in demand with the landed gentry, along with spun sugar sculptures, carved marzipan, and sweet doughs. Any or all of these dishes could be found at the center of every banquet table. Because of the demand, cooks found it necessary to devise new ways of presenting these dishes. Thus, jellied dishes molded in elaborate shapes were born. The earliest molds were carved from wood, but in time, metal (often copper) and ceramic molds in ever more elaborate shapes were commissioned and eventually became standard. They were easier to unmold, too.

it releases easily and cleanly from the mold.

There is, however, no restriction saying that only copper can be used. Glass or ceramic vessels of almost any size and shape can be repurposed for molding. When using these materials, choose a vessel that is not too thick as the density of the walls will inhibit the quick absorption of heat, making the gelatin tricky to unmold. I often use muffin cups, small dessert dishes, glassware, uniquely shaped bowls, or other pieces of tableware that might suit my serving plans. If you're planning to scoop the gelatin directly from the vessel rather than unmolding it whole, your options are nearly endless.

All of my recipes note the capacity of the mold, such as a 2-quart (2 L) or 6-cup (1.4 L) mold, required to safely hold the amount of gelatin in that recipe. Since the unmolded dish is often the star of the show, you want to use whatever you can to highlight its clarity and/or color. No matter what type of mold is used, the interior must be lightly coated with an unflavored cooking oil, such as vegetable, sunflower, or corn, or solid vegetable shortening. (I don't use cooking spray.) This makes removal of the finished dish quick and easy.

How to Use This Book

As you flip through the recipes in this book, your immediate reaction might be that they are too long and too complex to even think about making. This complexity comes from the fact that many of the dishes are layered or feature elaborate additions. However, each layer can easily be made and served on its own, with or without the additions. I personally love the dramatic appearance and experience of multiple layers and flavors brought together to create a spectacular look and taste. And while I love using glitter and gold leaf, they are just the WOW factor, so they can easily be omitted if you don't have them on hand. Since each layer and flavor can stand alone, I urge you to make each recipe your own with your preferred flavors and additions. Because gelatin-based recipes are, at their core, simple to make and fun to present, I think that the extra effort to create layers with the addition of edible glitter, gold or silver leaf, or other intoxicating additions can turn a simple recipe into a presentation that will stun your family or friends.

New to jelling? Wiggle down to business and start with Chapter 1: Super Simple Starter Jiggles. Each one is nothing more than tasty, jiggly fruit juice in a cup. Once you've got the hang of it, any of the sparkling desserts, decadent savories, or luxurious cocktails are yours to create. Let's get jiggly.

Getting Started

The Basics of Gelatin Making

Gelatin is pretty easy to work with once you get the hang of it, but there are some best practices you'll want to follow so you can unmold the most beautiful products each time.

TO PREP

STEP 1: Read the recipe. Always read through the recipe before you begin. This is particularly important with layered gelatin molds as there are often many steps and longer time periods for setting.

STEP 2: Choose a mold. To determine the volume of liquid that the mold will hold, fill the mold with water, then pour the water into a measuring cup; I usually start with a quart measure. Do this as many times as necessary to determine the volume of liquid your mold will hold and, consequently, how much gelatin you will need to set that specific amount of liquid. Of course, you do not have to use a mold every time. Sometimes, it is absolutely fine to make one type of gelatin in an attractive serving bowl.

STEP 3: Get organized. Gather all of the ingredients and put them into groups, keeping those for each layer separate. Organization ensures that you have all of the ingredients you need to proceed with the recipe.

STEP 4: Grease the mold. Coat the interior of the mold with an unflavored cooking oil, such as vegetable, sunflower, or corn, or solid vegetable shortening. This makes removal of the finished dish quick and easy. Plus, the quick removal prevents the gelatin itself from melting.

Place a small amount of oil or shortening in a shallow dish. Using a clean pastry brush, dip into the oil or shortening and coat the entire interior of the mold with a very light film. Take care that your brush goes up to and a slight bit over the edge of the mold (see page 8). When finished greasing the mold, check to make sure you have not left a pool of oil in the bottom or any bits of solid shortening anywhere on the interior.

Remember to grease the edge of the mold as well as the interior.

NOTE: If you plan to serve the gelatin directly from a mold, glass, or other vessel, it is not necessary to grease it. This is particularly the case with jelled drinks that can be served directly out of the vessel.

TO ASSEMBLE

STEP 5: Choose your gelling agent. Choose the gelatin you will be using, noting that sheet gelatin will yield a higher degree of clarity in a finished dish. Powdered gelatin will result in a firmer finished product. If you do not intend to unmold the jelly, you can use a bit less of either type for a softer product. The recipes in this book specify which type of gelatin is preferred in each.

- 1 gelatin sheet will set 3½ ounces (100 ml) liquid.
- 1 packet powdered gelatin (7 grams/about 2½ teaspoons) will set 2 cups (473 ml) liquid.
- 1 teaspoon agar agar powder will set 8 ounces (237 ml) liquid.
- 1 tablespoon (1½ g) agar agar flakes will set 8 ounces (237 ml) liquid.

Sheet gelatin should be cut into small pieces and placed in a container with just enough liquid (usually whatever liquid is going to be the base) to cover and set aside for about 10 minutes to bloom (soften). This is to ensure that the gelatin is softened enough to begin to melt slightly before you proceed with the next step to dissolve it fully in hot liquid. Most recipes call for the gelatin to be strained through a fine-mesh sieve. The sieve will catch any lumps of undissolved gelatin.

Powdered gelatin should be sprinkled over ¼ cup (59 ml) cold liquid and set aside to bloom for a specific time as given in each recipe. Unless a recipe says otherwise, add ¼ cup (59 ml) boiling liquid (or whatever hot liquid is used) and set aside until the gelatin granules have dissolved. Pour through a fine-mesh sieve into the remaining liquid unless the recipe indicates

Clockwise from top: sheet gelatin, powdered gelatin, agar agar powder, agar agar flakes

Edible glitter goes a long way. Less is more!

Straining the gelatin ensures a smooth, lumpless product.

Most gelatins need to be briefly prechilled before adding solids.

Solids won't sink to the bottom if the gelatin is set slightly before they're added.

otherwise. The sieve will catch any clumps of undissolved gelatin.

Agar agar should be mixed with 1 cup (237 ml) of liquid and stirred to incorporate. Then place in a small saucepan and bring to a boil over high heat. Lower the heat to a simmer and cook for 7 minutes before proceeding with a recipe.

STEP 6: Customize it. Combine any solids—such as fruit, spices, or glitter—with the gelatin mixture as indicated in the recipe. In the latter circumstance, carefully follow specific instructions.

STEP 7: Note the time and test for doneness. Refrigeration is required to set all gelatin recipes. Most recipes will give an exact time for a gelatin to set completely. The general rule of thumb for large molds is 6 to 24 hours. For small molds, the range is 3 to 24 hours. I generally allow at least 8 hours or, occasionally, up to 12 hours, to allow the gelatin to set securely before unmolding.

Occasionally, a recipe may call for placing the gelatin in the freezer for a short period of time, usually no more than 30 minutes, to speed up the setting process. Always, however, finish the process in the refrigerator because leaving your gelatin in the freezer will ruin the dish by causing the outer edges to freeze solid before the interior is set. I have tried, without much success, to allow a gelatin to set at room temperature. It has never worked satisfactorily for me.

The gelatin should jiggle yet firmly hold its shape when set.

There are two easy methods to check if the gelatin is set. The simplest is the **touch test**: Lightly touch the top with your fingertip. If the gelatin remains smooth, it is set. If it sticks to your fingertip, it has some time to go. This, unfortunately, also leaves a mark on the surface. Therefore, this testing method is best used when you are going to invert the molded gelatin onto a plate with the top side down so the blemish will not be seen.

The second method is the **jiggle test**: Gently move the mold back and forth—in other words, watch it jiggle! If the gelatin easily pulls away from the side, it is not set. At this point, I usually allow at least another hour to ensure that the gelatin has completely set.

Testing for doneness periodically is also the key to not overdrying your gelatins.

STEP 8: Layer it. When making a layered mold, it is important that each layer be set completely before a subsequent room-temperature layer is added. If not, the layers will meld together, and although edible, the neat design will be lost.

If a gelatin mixture has thickened too much to pour onto a set layer, return it to a small saucepan. Place over low heat and warm, stirring constantly, to loosen, about a minute or so. You don't want to let it get too hot. Remove from the heat and set aside to come to room temperature before using. Be patient—you don't want to risk melting the set layer when you pour it on top.

STEP 9: Cover it. If you plan to refrigerate the mold for more than 3 hours, it is a good idea to cover it completely with plastic film. Do not allow the film to touch the gelatin as it will stick and when unwrapping will lift off some gelatin. The plastic film will prevent the surface from setting too firmly and will also prevent the gelatin from absorbing refrigerator odors. The mold is best served within 24 hours (after that the edges may dry out and start to crack).

TO UNMOLD AND SERVE

STEP 10: Ready the bath. When ready to unmold the gelatin, place a pan or dish large enough to hold the mold on a work surface. Fill it about halfway with very hot water.

STEP 11: Unmold it. Remove the set mold from the refrigerator. Using your fingertips, gently push down around the edges of the gelatin to encourage it to begin releasing from the mold. Carefully dip the mold, gelatin side up, into the hot water, taking care that you don't allow the water to come up to the very top and into the mold. Let rest in the hot water for 2 to 3 seconds and no more than 30 seconds or it will begin to melt. The gelatin will very slightly begin to pull away from the mold.

STEP 12: Plate it. Remove the mold from the hot water and carefully dry it. Place a serving plate on top of the mold and quickly and gently turn it upside down while holding the plate flat. The gelatin will unmold and stick to the plate. If the plate surface is uneven or if you are concerned about placement, lightly wet the plate before unmolding. The wetness will allow the gelatin to be gently pushed into place. Follow recipe instructions for decoration or garnish.

STEP 13: Chill out. If not serving immediately, refrigerate until ready to serve or follow specific recipe instructions for serving.

Hold the plate flush against the mold while inverting.

A perfectly set gelatin is ready for a garnish.

In the front, a gelatin that has been properly chilled and tested. In the back, a gelatin that has been unmolded prematurely.

Cherries and Cream, 28
Orange Cream Terrazzo Dream, 80

Bloody Mary Brunch Shot, 153
Summer Melons, 49

Chapter 1

Super Simple Starter Jiggles

Apple Jiggle Juice

MAKES FOUR 8-OUNCE (237 ML) DESSERTS OR 1-QUART (1 L) MOLD

Not your usual juice box but essentially the same thing—just in jiggle form. You can easily double this recipe so the whole family can enjoy this refreshing treat. Without added sugar or paper wrapping, these are good for both you and the environment.

4 cups (1 L) apple juice or cider

2 packets (7 g each) unflavored gelatin powder, such as Knox brand

1 Place 1 cup (237 ml) of the apple juice in a medium heatproof bowl. Add the gelatin and set aside to bloom for 10 minutes.

2 Place the remaining juice in a small saucepan over medium heat. Bring to a gentle simmer.

3 Remove the juice from the heat and pour into the gelatin mixture, stirring until completely blended. Pour an equal portion of the juice mixture into each of four 8-ounce (237 ml) dessert cups or small dishes.

4 Place in the refrigerator and allow to chill until completely set, at least 3 hours.

5 Serve chilled.

Pure Fruit Gelatin

MAKES FOUR 8-OUNCE (237 ML) DESSERTS OR ONE 1-QUART (1 L) MOLD

Made from organic juice, this is a healthy alternative to presweetened gelatin desserts. Unsweetened juices are often much too tart to appeal to children, but you can still monitor the sugar intake by adding just enough to sweeten the flavor. If you are on a sugar-free diet, you can also use monk fruit sweetener, Splenda, or other sugar alternatives (see Note). A lively garnish of a gummy candy is that final touch that will appeal to the child in everyone.

- 4 cups (1 L) organic pure fruit juice
- 2 packets (7 g each) unflavored gelatin powder, such as Knox brand
- 2 tablespoons sugar or to taste (optional; see Note)
- Gummy candy for garnish (optional)

1 Place 1 cup (237 ml) of the juice in a medium heatproof bowl. Add the gelatin and set aside to bloom for 10 minutes.

2 Place the remaining 3 cups (710 ml) of juice in a small saucepan over medium heat. If using sugar to sweeten, add now and bring to a gentle simmer. Stir occasionally to ensure that the sugar has dissolved.

3 Remove from the heat and pour into the gelatin mixture, stirring to blend completely. When blended, pour an equal portion of the liquid into each of four 8-ounce (237 ml) dessert cups or small dishes.

4 Place in the refrigerator and allow to chill until completely set, at least 3 hours. If using a gummy candy garnish, place it on top of each jelly just before completely set, after about 90 minutes.

5 Serve chilled.

Note If you are using an unsweetened, organic fruit juice, you may need to add more than the suggested amount of sugar or sugar alternative to sweeten up the flavor to your taste. Start slowly as we suggest, adding a small amount at a time, to reach the desired degree of sweetness. Always make sure that the sugar or sweetener has dissolved before adding the flavored juice to the gelatin.

Lemonade Jiggler

MAKES SIX 8-OUNCE (237 ML) DESSERTS OR ONE 6-CUP (1.4 L) MOLD

There is nothing as delicious as homemade lemonade except, perhaps, a sparkling gelatin dessert made with it! Add a little gold leaf and it is a birthday kid's dream dessert (see Variation). Since lemonade is pale in color, it is nice to add some type of garnish (gummy or other candies or candied or fresh fruit), particularly when making it for children. If you want to save time, use premade lemonade in place of making it yourself and save the mint for a garnish.

4 cups (1 L) water

2 packets (7 g each) unflavored gelatin powder, such as Knox brand

1 cup (200 g) sugar or to taste

1 cup (237 ml) fresh lemon juice, strained of all pulp

½ cup (15 g) fresh mint leaves, plus extra mint sprigs for garnish (optional)

1 Place 1 cup (237 ml) of the water in a medium heatproof bowl. Add the gelatin and set aside to bloom for 10 minutes.

2 Combine the sugar with 3 cups (710 ml) of the remaining water in a medium saucepan over medium heat. Bring to a simmer and heat, stirring occasionally, until the sugar has dissolved completely, about 3 minutes. Add the lemon juice and mint leaves, if using, stirring to blend.

3 Remove the juice mixture from the heat and add the gelatin, stirring constantly to dissolve the gelatin completely. Taste and, if necessary, stir in additional sugar while the mixture remains hot enough to dissolve it. Taste again and, if too tart, add just enough sugar to achieve the desired degree of sweetness. Set aside at room temperature to allow the mint to infuse the lemonade, about 30 minutes.

4 Strain the mixture through a fine-mesh sieve into a clean bowl, discarding the mint. Divide the mixture equally among six 8-ounce (237 ml) dessert cups or small dishes. Transfer to the refrigerator and chill until completely set, at least 3 hours.

5 Serve chilled, garnished with a mint sprig or any other garnish you desire.

Variation **Glittery Gold Leaf Lemon Jiggler:** If you want to add some sparkle with edible gold leaf, add it before dividing the gelatin into individual portions. Set the bowl of lemonade gelatin into a larger ice-filled bowl. Break the gold leaf into small pieces and add the gold leaf to the mixture, stirring constantly, until the gold leaf breaks into even smaller pieces and the gelatin begins to set, about 15 minutes. As you stir and the gelatin thickens, the gold leaf should remain suspended throughout the jelly. At this point you can divide the jelly into individual portions (use glass vessels so the gold leaf can shine through) and chill and serve as directed.

Pomegranate Jelly

MAKES FOUR ½-CUP (118 ML) DESSERTS OR ONE 2-CUP (473 ML) MOLD

Pomegranate is good for us and is oh so refreshing. Topped with yogurt, it makes a deliciously healthy treat for both children and adults!

2 cups (473 ml) pomegranate juice

1 packet (7 g) unflavored gelatin powder, such as Knox brand

2 tablespoons sugar

½ cup (60 g) pomegranate arils (optional)

2 tablespoons chopped fresh mint leaves (optional)

¼ cup (60 g) vanilla yogurt or frozen yogurt for serving (optional)

Make the Pomegranate Gelatin

1 Place ½ cup (118 ml) of the pomegranate juice in a small bowl. Add the gelatin and set aside to bloom for 10 minutes.

2 Place the remaining 1½ cups (355 ml) of juice and the sugar in a small saucepan over medium heat. Bring to a gentle simmer.

3 Remove from the heat and add the gelatin mixture, stirring to blend completely.

Add the Arils and Mint, If Using

1 Transfer the pomegranate gelatin to the refrigerator and chill just until beginning to set, about 30 minutes. Remove the almost-set jelly from the refrigerator and stir the arils and mint into it.

2 Spoon the gelatin mixture into each of four ½ cup (118 ml) dessert cups or small dishes (see Note). Transfer to the refrigerator and chill until set, at least 3 hours or no more than 24 hours.

3 Serve chilled with a dollop of vanilla yogurt on top, if desired.

Note If you'd like to unmold it as pictured, just remember to lightly grease your mold with neutral oil before spooning in the gelatin. See the instructions on page 13.

Chapter 2

Sweet Things

Cherries and Cream

MAKES ONE 1-QUART (1 L) MOLD

I absolutely love the pure, clean flavor of Filthy Black Cherry Syrup. Although it is normally used in cocktails, the intense flavor inspired me to come up with a way to let it shine using gelatin. I've always liked the combination of cherry and vanilla so that was my starting point. This recipe is at its best made with fresh Bing cherries, but you can substitute fine-quality canned black cherries when cherries are not in season. The combination of the creamy layer with the slightly tart cherries is the perfect marriage of textures and flavors.

Vegetable oil for greasing the mold

CREAM SODA GELATIN

2 packets (7 g each) unflavored gelatin powder, such as Knox brand

2 tablespoons superfine sugar

2 cups (473 ml) clear cream soda, such as D&G Genuine Jamaican Cream Soda (see Notes)

1 teaspoon edible glitter

2 tablespoons Filthy Black Cherry Syrup (see Notes)

CHERRY GELATIN

⅓ cup (79 ml) Filthy Black Cherry Syrup plus 3 tablespoons (45 ml) for coloring

⅓ cup (79 ml) cold water

2 packets (7 g each) unflavored gelatin powder, such as Knox brand

One 14-ounce (397 g) can sweetened condensed milk

1 cup (237 ml) boiling water

1 tablespoon pure vanilla extract

1 cup (152 g) diced pitted fresh Bing cherries

About 1 cup (about 125 g) chilled Bing cherries with stems attached for garnish

Prep the Mold

Lightly coat the interior of a 1-quart (1 L) mold with vegetable oil. Set aside.

(continued)

Make the Cream Soda Gelatin

1 Combine the gelatin and sugar in a medium saucepan, stirring to blend. Add the cream soda and stir to incorporate the gelatin and sugar. Set aside to bloom for 10 minutes.

2 Place the gelatin mixture over low heat and cook, stirring constantly, until the gelatin and sugar have dissolved, about 3 minutes. Pour half of the mixture into the prepared mold and transfer the mold to the refrigerator to chill until semi-firm, about 15 minutes. Reserve the remaining mixture in the saucepan.

3 Remove the gelatin from the refrigerator and stir in the edible glitter. Immediately return to the refrigerator and let set until just firm enough to hold its shape, about 40 minutes.

4 Add the cherry syrup to the reserved cream soda mixture, stirring to blend well. Remove the mold from the refrigerator and carefully spoon this cherry–cream soda mixture over it. Return the mold to the refrigerator and let set until almost solid, about 40 minutes.

Make the Cherry Gelatin

1 Combine the cherry syrup and the cold water in a medium saucepan, stirring to blend. Sprinkle the gelatin over the mixture and set aside to bloom for 10 minutes.

2 Place the sweetened condensed milk in a small heatproof bowl. Add the boiling water along with the vanilla extract, stirring to blend well. Add the condensed milk mixture to the bloomed gelatin mixture and place over low heat. Cook, stirring constantly, until the gelatin has dissolved, about 4 minutes. Set aside at room temperature to cool completely, about 1 hour.

3 Divide the condensed milk mixture into 2 equal portions. Add ½ cup (76 g) of the pitted cherries to one portion; reserve the other portion.

Build the Layers

1 Remove the mold from the refrigerator and carefully pour the pitted cherry mixture over the cream soda layer (which will now be set). Return the mold to the refrigerator and chill until the cherry gelatin is almost set, about 30 minutes.

2 While the mold chills, add the remaining 3 tablespoons (45 ml) of cherry syrup to the reserved condensed milk mixture to tint it a darker pink. Stir in the remaining ½ cup (76 g) of pitted cherries. After the first portion of cherry gelatin is firm enough to hold its shape, carefully spoon this mixture over it.

3 Tightly cover the entire mold with plastic film and return it to the refrigerator. Chill until firm, at least 6 hours or no more than 24 hours.

Unmold It

1 Remove the mold from the refrigerator. Remove and discard the plastic film. Place the mold in a bowl filled with hot water to come up to but not over the edge. Hold for 15 to 30 seconds to loosen. Watch carefully as you do not want the gelatin to begin melting.

2 Remove the mold from the water and wipe the exterior dry. Place a serving plate over the mold and invert the mold onto it. The gelatin should pop right out. If desired, garnish the top of the gelatin with the chilled Bing cherries, their stems pointed upward.

3 Serve immediately.

Notes I use D&G Genuine Jamaican Cream Soda for this recipe because I love its flavor and it is crystal clear. If you use another brand, be certain that it is absolutely colorless or it will distort the clarity of the Cream Soda Gelatin. D&G Genuine Jamaican Cream Soda is available online.

Filthy Black Cherry Syrup is available online through filthyfood.com.

Peachy Keen Pretzel Mold

MAKES ONE 8-INCH (20 CM) SPRINGFORM LOAF MOLD

This recipe has been a staple at our family parties for as far back as I can remember. The combination of salty, sweet, creamy, and crunchy makes it extremely hard to say no to a second slice. Traditionally it's made with strawberries—feel free to substitute fresh strawberries and strawberry puree if you like.

I like to use a springform loaf pan so that the layers shine. You can certainly use a 6-cup (1.4 L) mold of any shape. The pretzel layer can be quite crumbly, and the loaf can go from perfection to a bit of a mess very quickly. After you unmold the gelatin, it is best to leave it on the bottom plate of the springform pan so it remains intact. But if you are feeling lucky, you can run a large metal spatula between the pretzel layer and the bottom plate. Then, very carefully transfer the whole loaf to a serving platter.

Vegetable oil for greasing the springform pan

PRETZEL CRUST

2 cups (250 g) crushed salted pretzels

3 tablespoons (36 g) granulated sugar

1 teaspoon ground cinnamon

¾ cup (1½ sticks/170 g) unsalted butter, melted

CREAM CHEESE LAYER

8 ounces (227 g) cream cheese, at room temperature

8 ounces (227 g) Cool Whip, thawed

1 cup (127 g) confectioners' sugar

1 teaspoon pure vanilla extract

PEACH NECTAR GELATIN

2 cups (473 ml) organic peach nectar

2½ sheets gelatin, broken into pieces

2 firm but ripe peaches, peeled, pitted, and cut into thin slices

CREAM SODA GELATIN

2 cups (473 ml) clear cream soda, such as D&G Genuine Jamaican Cream Soda (see Note)

2½ sheets gelatin, broken into pieces

Prep the Mold

1 Preheat the oven to 350°F (177°C). Lightly coat the sides of an 8-inch (20 cm) springform loaf pan with vegetable oil.

2 Lightly coat the bottom plate of the pan with vegetable oil, then attach the ring to it. Set aside.

Make the Pretzel Crust

1 Combine the pretzel crumbs with the granulated sugar and cinnamon in a medium mixing bowl. Add the melted butter and stir to incorporate completely.

2 Pour the pretzel mixture into the prepared pan. Using your fingertips, press the mixture onto the bottom of the pan, keeping it in a neat, compact layer.

3 Transfer to the preheated oven and bake until slightly dry and firm, 8 minutes. Remove from the oven and place on a wire rack to cool.

Make the Cream Cheese Layer

1 Place the cream cheese, Cool Whip, confectioners' sugar, and vanilla in a medium mixing bowl. Using a handheld electric mixer, beat until very smooth.

2 Spoon the cream cheese mixture over the cooled pretzel crust. Using an offset spatula, smooth the cream cheese out to an even layer, completely covering the pretzel crust.

3 Transfer the pan to the refrigerator and allow the cream cheese mixture to chill thoroughly, 1 hour.

Make the Peach Nectar Gelatin

1 Place 1 cup (237 ml) of the peach nectar in a small saucepan. Add the gelatin pieces and set aside to bloom for 10 minutes.

2 Add the remaining 1 cup (237 ml) of nectar to the bloomed gelatin and place the saucepan over low heat. Warm, stirring occasionally, until the gelatin has dissolved completely, about 10 minutes. Remove from the heat, pour through a fine-mesh sieve into a clean bowl, and set aside to cool to room temperature.

(continued)

3 When the peach nectar mixture has cooled, remove the mold from the refrigerator and pour the peach layer over the cream cheese layer. Immediately return to the refrigerator and chill until firm, about 1 hour.

Make the Cream Soda Gelatin

1 Place 1 cup (237 ml) of the cream soda into a small saucepan. Add the gelatin pieces to the soda and set aside to bloom for 10 minutes.

2 Add the remaining 1 cup (237 ml) of cream soda to the bloomed gelatin and place the saucepan over low heat. Warm, stirring occasionally, until the gelatin has dissolved completely, about 10 minutes. Remove from the heat, pour through a fine-mesh sieve into a clean bowl, and set aside to cool to room temperature.

Build the Layers

1 When the peach nectar layer has set, remove the mold from the refrigerator and carefully place the peach slices on top, overlapping them slightly. Carefully pour the cream soda mixture over the peaches to cover completely.

2 Tightly cover the entire mold with plastic film and return it to the refrigerator. Chill until completely set, at least 4 hours or no more than 24 hours.

Unmold It

1 Remove the mold from the refrigerator. Remove and discard the plastic film. Unlatch and remove the rim of the mold. Leaving the bottom plate in place (see headnote), transfer the mold to a serving board or platter.

2 Serve immediately, cut into neat slices.

Note D&G Genuine Jamaican Cream Soda is available online. If you choose another brand, please be certain that it is absolutely clear in color, or it will distort the clarity of the cream soda layer.

Creamy Cocoa

MAKES ONE 5-CUP (1.2 L) MOLD

I absolutely love a cup of hot chocolate in the winter, but it really holds no appeal for me come the summer months. So, what to do in warmer weather? I simply turned my favorite wintertime treat into a year-round dessert complete with marshmallows. The one trick here is getting the lighter-than-air marshmallows to stay put in the setting chocolate gelatin. Some patience is required! When complete, the cream layer will be on the top of the cocoa layer and the marshmallows will be floating throughout.

Vegetable oil for greasing the mold

CREAM GELATIN

1 cup (237 ml) heavy cream

1¼ teaspoons unflavored gelatin powder, such as Knox brand

¼ cup (50 g) sugar

½ vanilla bean, split

1 cup (2 g) large marshmallows

COCOA GELATIN

4 cups (1 L) heavy cream

2 packets (7 g each) unflavored gelatin powder, such as Knox brand

1 vanilla bean, halved crosswise, each half split

1¼ cups (125 g) Milk Chocolate Swiss Miss Hot Chocolate Mix

2 cups (4 g) large marshmallows

Shaved chocolate for garnish

Prep the Mold

Lightly coat the interior of a 5-cup (1.2 L) ring mold with the vegetable oil. Set aside.

Make the Cream Gelatin

1 Place the cream in a small saucepan. Sprinkle the gelatin over the top and set aside to bloom for 10 minutes.

(continued)

2 Stir in the sugar along with the ½ vanilla bean. Place over low heat and warm, stirring occasionally, until the gelatin and sugar have completely dissolved, about 5 minutes. Continue to cook, stirring occasionally, at a bare simmer to infuse the vanilla scent into the cream, 15 minutes.

3 Remove from the heat and pour through a fine-mesh sieve into the prepared mold. Place the marshmallows on top of the cream mixture, keeping them toward the center of the ring. Transfer to the refrigerator and let set, about 1 hour. Check from time to time to make sure that the marshmallows are settling into the cream; if they are floating up to the surface, push them down as necessary.

Make the Cocoa Gelatin

1 Place 2 cups (473 ml) of the cream in a medium saucepan. Sprinkle the gelatin powder over the top. Set aside to bloom for 10 minutes.

2 Transfer the mixture in the saucepan to low heat and stir in the remaining 2 cups (473 ml) of cream along with the split vanilla bean. Cook, stirring occasionally, until the gelatin has completely dissolved, about 5 minutes. Continue to cook at a bare simmer to infuse the vanilla scent into the cream, 15 minutes.

3 Whisk the cocoa mix into the gelatin mixture and continue to cook until it has dissolved completely. Remove from the heat and pour the mixture through a fine-mesh sieve into a large bowl. Transfer to the refrigerator and let chill, stirring occasionally, until just beginning to thicken, about 1 hour.

Build the Layers

1 Pour about three-quarters of the thickened cocoa mixture over the cream layer. Randomly insert the large marshmallows throughout the cocoa layer. Return to the refrigerator and let set until firm, about another hour.

2 Remove from the refrigerator and pour the remaining cocoa mixture over the marshmallow layer. Tightly cover the entire mold with plastic film and return it to the refrigerator. Chill until firm, about 4 hours or no more than 24 hours.

Unmold It

1 Remove the mold from the refrigerator. Remove and discard the plastic film. Place the mold in a bowl filled with hot water to come up to but not over the edge. Hold for 15 to 30 seconds to loosen. Watch carefully as you do not want the gelatin to begin melting.

2 Remove the mold from the water and wipe the exterior dry. Place a serving plate over the mold and invert the mold onto it. The gelatin should pop right out. If desired, garnish the top with shaved chocolate.

3 Serve immediately, cut into wedges.

Polka Dot Peaches 'n' Cream

MAKES ONE 6-CUP (1.4 L) MOLD

I know, I know—this creamy white gelatin studded with peach polka dots seems a bit intricate to create. But it really is quite easy; it just takes a little bit of extra patience. It is very important to have the mold ice-cold so that the polka dots will stick to it. You do need 1½-inch (3.8 cm) round cookie cutters to cut out the polka dots. However, if you don't have them, you can use small glasses to cut out similar-size circles. The finished gelatin is so delightful to look at and yummy to eat so please give it a try.

Vegetable oil for greasing the mold and baking sheet

CREAM GELATIN

6 cups (1.4 L) heavy cream

¾ cup (150 g) sugar

1 vanilla bean, split lengthwise

¼ cup (59 ml) water

3 packets (7 g each) unflavored gelatin powder, such as Knox brand

PEACH GELATIN

2 cups (473 ml) organic peach nectar

1 packet (7 g) unflavored gelatin powder, such as Knox brand

2 peaches, peeled, pitted, and chopped

Prep the Molds

1 Lightly coat the interior of a 6-cup (1.4 L) mold with vegetable oil. Transfer the greased mold to the freezer.

2 Lightly coat a 9½ × 13-inch (24 × 33 cm) rimmed baking sheet with vegetable oil. Set aside.

(continued)

Make the Cream Gelatin

1 Combine the cream and sugar in a medium saucepan. Scrape the seeds from the vanilla bean into the cream, then add the scraped bean to the mix. Place over medium heat and bring to a simmer. Immediately remove from the heat, cover, and set aside to steep for 15 minutes.

2 Place the water in a small bowl. Sprinkle the gelatin over the top and set aside to bloom for 10 minutes.

3 Return the cream to medium-high heat, uncover, and bring to a bare simmer. Remove from the heat, add the reserved gelatin mixture, and stir until the gelatin powder has dissolved completely. Pour the mixture through a fine-mesh sieve into a clean bowl and set aside to come to room temperature.

Make the Peach Gelatin

1 Combine 1 cup (237 ml) of the peach nectar with the gelatin in a small saucepan. Set aside to bloom for 10 minutes.

2 Place the saucepan over low heat and add the remaining 1 cup (237 ml) of peach nectar. Cook, stirring frequently, until the gelatin has completely dissolved, about 3 minutes.

3 Remove from the heat and pour the mixture through a fine-mesh sieve onto the reserved greased baking sheet. Transfer to the refrigerator and let set until very firm, about 1 hour.

Make the Polka Dots

1 When ready to unmold the peach gelatin, lightly grease a clean, flat work surface, such as a marble pastry slab. Invert the baking sheet onto the greased surface, bottom side up, and lightly tap around the bottom to unmold the peach gelatin. Because the sheet was greased, the gelatin should pop right out. If it doesn't, place a wet, hot dish towel over it for a few seconds.

2 Using 1½-inch (3.8 cm) round cookie cutters, cut out 8 to 10 gelatin circles. (Reserve any leftover peach gelatin in the refrigerator for use in the following steps.)

3 Remove the greased mold from the freezer. Quickly and carefully stick gelatin circles onto the insides of the mold in a random pattern. Immediately return the mold to the freezer to allow the circles to adhere, about 10 minutes.

Build the Layers

1 Remove the mold from the freezer and pour in the cooled cream mixture. Transfer to the refrigerator until firm, about 2 hours.

2 Place the reserved peach gelatin in a small saucepan over low heat. Add the chopped peaches and cook, stirring constantly, until the gelatin has melted, about 3 minutes.

3 Remove the mold from the refrigerator. Using a round tablespoon, carefully scoop out about 1 cup (237 ml) of the firm cream gelatin from the center of the mold, leaving at least 1 inch (2.5 cm) of the cream gelatin around the perimeter of the circle and save for a snack or discard. Carefully spoon the peach gelatin into the cavity.

4 Tightly wrap the entire mold with plastic film and return it to the refrigerator. Let chill until the cream gelatin is quite firm, but still a wee bit jiggly, about 4 hours or no more than 24 hours.

Unmold It

1 Remove the mold from the refrigerator. Remove and discard the plastic film. Place the mold in a bowl filled with hot water to come up to but not over the edge. Hold for 15 to 30 seconds to loosen. Watch carefully as you do not want the gelatin to begin melting.

2 Remove the mold from the water and wipe the exterior dry. Place a serving plate over the mold and invert the mold onto it. The gelatin should pop right out.

3 Serve immediately, cut into slices.

Neato-Politan

MAKES ONE 3-CUP (710 ML) MOLD

Growing up in an Italian household, Neapolitan ice cream was one of my favorite desserts. When I began playing with gelatin, I did a little research on the standard combination of chocolate, strawberry, and pistachio ice creams and found that it is not Italian at all but a German invention. Somewhere along the way vanilla replaced the pistachio, and Italian Americans adopted the dessert.

As with the ice cream, this gelatin, when unmolded, produces three layers of color. The chocolate layer will be on the bottom, the strawberry in the center, and the vanilla on top.

Vegetable oil for greasing the mold

VANILLA AND CHOCOLATE GELATINS

2 cups (473 ml) heavy cream

½ vanilla bean, split

1 packet (7 g) unflavored gelatin powder, such as Knox brand

½ cup (100 g) sugar

1 tablespoon unsweetened cocoa powder

STRAWBERRY GELATIN

1 cup (170 g) chopped fresh strawberries

1 tablespoon fresh lemon juice

2 tablespoons sugar

1 packet (7 g) unflavored gelatin powder, such as Knox brand

Prep the Mold

Lightly coat the interior of a 3-cup (710 ml) mold with vegetable oil. Set aside.

Make the Vanilla Gelatin

1 Place the cream in a medium saucepan. Scrape the vanilla seeds from the bean into the cream and add the bean, too. Sprinkle the packet of gelatin over the top and set aside to bloom for 10 minutes.

2 Add the sugar to the vanilla cream mixture and place over low heat. Cook, stirring frequently, until the gelatin and sugar are dissolved completely.

3 Remove from the heat and pour 1 cup (237 ml) of the vanilla cream mixture into a bowl (reserve the rest). Place the bowl in the freezer until the mixture begins to thicken, about 20 minutes. (The quick chill will help keep the vanilla seeds suspended in the cream.)

4 Remove from the freezer and pour the thickening mixture into the prepared mold. Return to the freezer until very firm, about another 20 minutes.

Make the Chocolate Gelatin

1 Pour the reserved 1 cup (237 ml) of vanilla cream mixture into a small saucepan. Place over low heat and whisk in the cocoa powder. Cook, whisking constantly, at a bare simmer until the cocoa has blended into the cream, about 15 minutes.

2 Remove from the heat and pour through a fine-mesh sieve into a small bowl. Set aside to come to room temperature.

Make the Strawberry Gelatin

1 Combine the strawberries with the lemon juice and sugar in a small saucepan. Place over medium heat and bring to a simmer. Lower the heat and cook at a bare simmer, stirring frequently, until the strawberries are very soft and the sugar has dissolved, about 15 minutes.

2 Remove from the heat and sprinkle the gelatin over the top. Set aside to bloom for 10 minutes.

3 Return the strawberries to low heat and cook, stirring constantly, until the gelatin has dissolved completely, about 4 minutes.

4 Remove from the heat and pour into a small bowl. Place in the freezer until the mixture has begun to thicken, about 20 minutes.

(continued)

Build the Layers

1 Remove the mold from the freezer and carefully spoon the strawberry mixture over the set vanilla layer. Place the mold in the refrigerator and chill until the strawberry layer is firm, about 45 minutes.

2 Remove the mold from the refrigerator and carefully spoon the cooled chocolate cream mixture over the set strawberry layer.

3 Tightly wrap the entire mold with plastic film and return it to the refrigerator. Let chill until firm, about 4 hours or no more than 24 hours.

Unmold It

1 Remove the mold from the refrigerator. Remove and discard the plastic film. Place the mold in a bowl filled with hot water to come up to but not over the edge. Hold for 15 to 30 seconds to loosen. Watch carefully as you do not want the gelatin to begin melting.

2 Remove the mold from the water and wipe the exterior dry. Place a serving plate over the mold and invert the mold onto it. The gelatin should pop right out.

3 Serve immediately, cut into slices.

Apple-Cinnamon Toast Panna Cotta

MAKES EIGHT 6-OUNCE (177 ML) DESSERT CUPS

Just a few years ago, you could not find panna cotta on any American menu, except for at a very few Italian restaurants. Now, it is often featured as a dessert and, sometimes, as a savory appetizer. Panna cotta translates to "cooked cream," and that it is exactly what it is—with gelatin added to make a rich, jiggly dish. This recipe combines apple cider and crunchy cinnamon toast cereal (an American kids' favorite—and one of mine, too) with this somewhat fancy Italian pudding, making a crispy, creamy combination. I can guarantee that it will bring out the kid in even the most sophisticated diner. You don't need the compote to garnish, but it does bring the whole dish up a notch.

When unmolded, the apple cider layer will be the top layer with the panna cotta layer forming the base.

Vegetable oil for greasing the molds

APPLE CIDER GELATIN

1 cup (237 ml) apple cider

2 tablespoons sugar

1 tablespoon ground cinnamon

1 packet (7 g) unflavored gelatin powder, such as Knox brand

1 teaspoon edible gold glitter

CINNAMON TOAST PANNA COTTA

4 cups (1 L) heavy cream

2 cups (40 g) Cinnamon Toast Crunch cereal

½ cup (100 g) sugar

½ vanilla bean, split lengthwise

3 tablespoons (45 ml) water

1 packet (7 g) unflavored gelatin powder, such as Knox brand

APPLE COMPOTE (OPTIONAL)

1 pound (454 g) Granny Smith or other tart apples, peeled, cored, and chopped

1 tablespoon light brown sugar

1 tablespoon apple cider

1 teaspoon fresh lemon juice

½ teaspoon ground cinnamon or nutmeg

(continued)

Prep the Molds

Lightly coat the interior of eight 6-ounce (177 ml) dessert cups with vegetable oil. Set aside.

Make the Apple Cider Gelatin

1 Combine the apple cider, sugar, and cinnamon in a medium saucepan. Sprinkle the gelatin evenly over the top and set aside to bloom for 10 minutes.

2 Place the saucepan over medium heat and bring to a simmer, stirring frequently until the sugar has dissolved. Remove from the heat and set aside to cool to room temperature.

3 When the apple cider mixture begins to cool and thicken slightly, add the edible glitter, stirring until the glitter is evenly distributed throughout.

4 Pour an equal portion of the cider mixture into each of the prepared cups. Transfer to the refrigerator until firm, about 1 hour.

Make the Cinnamon Toast Panna Cotta

1 Combine the heavy cream and cereal in a medium mixing bowl. Cover and refrigerate to allow the cereal flavor to infuse the cream, about 4 hours.

2 Strain the cream through a fine-mesh sieve into a medium saucepan. Add the sugar and, using a small sharp knife, scrape the seeds from the vanilla bean into the mixture. Add the scraped bean as well. Place over medium heat and bring to a bare simmer. Remove from the heat, cover, and allow to steep for 15 minutes.

3 Meanwhile, place the water in a small bowl. Sprinkle the gelatin on top and set aside to bloom, about 10 minutes.

4 Uncover the steeped cream, return the pan to medium heat, and bring to a bare simmer. Immediately remove from the heat and add the bloomed gelatin, stirring constantly. Remove and discard the vanilla bean. Set aside the vanilla cream mixture to come to room temperature.

Build the Layers

1 Remove the cups from the refrigerator. Pour an equal portion of the panna cotta mixture over the cider layer in each cup.

2 Tightly cover each cup with plastic film. Transfer to the refrigerator until the panna cotta is set, but still slightly jiggly, at least 3 hours and no more than 24 hours.

Make the Apple Compote (If Using)

1 Combine the apples with the brown sugar, cider, lemon juice, and cinnamon in a small saucepan over medium heat. Bring to a simmer, stirring occasionally. Lower the heat and cook, stirring frequently, until the apples have softened slightly and the flavors have blended, about 12 minutes.

2 Remove from the heat and transfer to a food-safe container with a lid. Allow to cool, then refrigerate until ready to serve (it will keep for up to 3 days).

Unmold Them

1 Remove the dessert cups from the refrigerator. Remove and discard the plastic film. Working with one at a time, place a dessert cup in a bowl filled with hot water to come up to but not over the edge. Hold for 15 to 30 seconds to loosen. Watch carefully as you do not want the gelatin to begin melting. Remove the cup from the water and wipe the exterior dry.

2 Place a small dessert plate over the dessert cup and invert the cup onto it. The gelatin should pop right out. Repeat with the remaining cups.

3 If using, carefully dollop about a tablespoon of the compote on top or at the side of each dessert. Alternatively, sprinkle a bit of ground cinnamon over the top and around the plate. Serve immediately.

Summer Melons

MAKES ONE 3-CUP (710 ML) MOLD

Not only is this gelatin mold beautiful to look at with its pale, almost translucent layers, it is incredibly refreshing. When choosing a mold for it, since the colors are so pale, make sure that each layer is clearly divided so that each color is distinct. It can easily be doubled and served at a summer lunch or barbecue—simply use a 6-cup (1.4 L) mold.

Vegetable oil for greasing the mold

CANTALOUPE GELATIN

1 cup (227 g) diced cantaloupe

½ cup (118 ml) white grape juice

1 packet (7 g) unflavored powered gelatin, such as Knox brand

Juice of ½ lemon

WATERMELON GELATIN

1 cup (210 g) diced watermelon

½ cup (118 ml) white grape juice

1 packet (7 g) unflavored powered gelatin, such as Knox brand

Juice of ½ lime

HONEYDEW GELATIN

1 cup (227 g) diced honeydew

½ cup (118 ml) white grape juice

¼ cup (50 g) sugar

Juice of 1 lime

¼ teaspoon edible iridescent glitter

1 packet (7 g) unflavored powered gelatin, such as Knox brand

Prep the Mold

Lightly coat a 3-cup (710 ml) mold with vegetable oil. Set aside.

Make the Cantaloupe Gelatin

1 Place the cantaloupe and grape juice in a blender jar and blend to a smooth puree. Pour the puree through a fine-mesh sieve into a small saucepan. Sprinkle the gelatin over the top and set aside to bloom for 10 minutes.

(continued)

2 Place the cantaloupe mixture in the saucepan over low heat and cook, stirring frequently, until the gelatin has dissolved completely, about 4 minutes.

3 Stir in the lemon juice and pour into a small bowl. Transfer to the freezer and, stirring occasionally, chill to thicken slightly, about 30 minutes.

4 Pour the cantaloupe puree into the prepared mold and place in the refrigerator. Chill until firm, about 1 hour.

Make the Watermelon Gelatin

1 Place the watermelon and grape juice in a blender jar and blend to a smooth puree. Pour the puree through a fine-mesh sieve into a small saucepan. Sprinkle the gelatin over the top and set aside to bloom for 10 minutes.

2 Place the watermelon mixture in the saucepan over low heat and cook, stirring frequently, until the gelatin has dissolved completely, about 4 minutes.

3 Stir in the lime juice and pour into a small bowl. Transfer to the freezer and, stirring occasionally, chill to thicken slightly, about 30 minutes.

4 Pour the chilled watermelon layer over the set cantaloupe layer in the prepared mold and place in the refrigerator. Chill until firm, about 1 hour.

Make the Honeydew Gelatin

1 Place the honeydew and grape juice in a blender jar and blend to a smooth puree. Pour the puree through a fine-mesh sieve into a small saucepan. Sprinkle the gelatin over the top and set aside to bloom for 10 minutes.

2 Add the sugar, place over low heat, and cook, stirring frequently, until the sugar and gelatin have dissolved completely, about 5 minutes.

3 Stir in the lime juice and pour into a small bowl. Transfer to the freezer and, stirring occasionally, chill to thicken slightly, about 30 minutes.

Build the Layers

1 Remove the honeydew mixture from the freezer and stir in the glitter, making sure it is evenly suspended throughout. Pour the honeydew mixture over the set watermelon layer.

2 Tightly wrap the entire mold with plastic film and return it to the refrigerator. Let chill until firm, about 3 hours or no more than 24 hours.

Unmold It

1 Remove the mold from the refrigerator. Remove and discard the plastic film. Place the mold in a bowl filled with hot water to come up to but not over the edge. Hold for 15 to 30 seconds to loosen. Watch carefully as you do not want the gelatin to begin melting.

2 Remove the mold from the water and wipe the exterior dry. Place a serving plate over the mold and invert the mold onto it. The gelatin should pop right out.

3 Serve immediately, cut into slices.

Blackberries, Chestnuts, and Cream, Oh My!

MAKES ONE 6-CUP (1.4 L) MOLD

This is a very unusual combination that results in a luscious, creamy mix. The tartness of the fresh blackberries highlights the rich creaminess of the candied chestnuts. The warm spices in the chestnut cream add another layer of intrigue that is just a wee bit unknowable. When unmolded, the chestnut layer will be on the bottom and the blackberry layer on the top.

Vegetable oil for greasing the mold

BLACKBERRY GELATIN

2 pints (about 680 g) fresh blackberries

¼ cup (59 ml) fresh orange juice, strained

2 tablespoons sugar

1 heaping teaspoon unflavored gelatin powder, such as Knox brand

CHESTNUT GELATIN

1 jar (415 g) candied chestnuts in syrup

2 cups (473 ml) heavy cream

1 teaspoon ground cinnamon

Pinch of grated nutmeg

1 packet (7 g) unflavored gelatin powder, such as Knox brand

1 pint (340 g) blackberries for garnish (optional)

Prep the Mold

Lightly coat the interior of a 6-cup (1.4 L) ring mold with vegetable oil. Set aside.

Make the Blackberry Gelatin

1 Place the blackberries, orange juice, and sugar in a medium saucepan over medium heat. Bring to a boil, then immediately lower the heat and cook at a gentle simmer until the mixture thickens and coats the back of a spoon, 30 minutes.

2 Remove the blackberry mixture from the heat and strain through a fine-mesh sieve into a clean small saucepan, discarding the solids.

3 Transfer ½ cup (118 ml) of the blackberry mixture to a small bowl (reserve the rest in the saucepan). Sprinkle the gelatin over the top of the mixture in the bowl and set aside to bloom for 10 minutes.

4 Add the gelatin mixture to the blackberry mixture in the pan and transfer to medium heat. Cook, stirring constantly, until the gelatin has dissolved completely, about 4 minutes. Remove from the heat and set aside to cool to room temperature.

5 Pour the cooled blackberry mixture into the prepared mold and transfer to the refrigerator to set until firm, about 3 hours.

Make the Chestnut Gelatin

1 Place the chestnuts along with their syrup in a blender jar and process on high until they form a thick, smooth puree, about 5 minutes.

2 Place the heavy cream in a medium saucepan. Add the chestnut puree, cinnamon, and nutmeg and place over medium heat. Cook, whisking constantly, until hot and well blended, about 3 minutes.

3 Turn off the heat and sprinkle the gelatin over the top of the chestnut mixture in the saucepan and set aside to bloom for 10 minutes.

4 Return the saucepan with the chestnut mixture to low heat and cook, stirring constantly, until the gelatin has dissolved completely, about 4 minutes. Remove from the heat and set aside to come to room temperature.

Build the Layers

1 Remove the mold from the refrigerator and carefully pour the cooled chestnut mixture over the top of the blackberry layer.

2 Tightly wrap the entire mold with plastic film and return it to the refrigerator. Let chill until firm, about 4 hours or no more than 24 hours.

(continued)

Unmold It

1 Remove the mold from the refrigerator. Remove and discard the plastic film. Place the mold in a bowl filled with hot water to come up to but not over the edge. Hold for 15 to 30 seconds to loosen. Watch carefully as you do not want the gelatin to begin melting.

2 Remove the mold from the water and wipe the exterior dry. Place a serving plate or small cake stand over the mold and invert the mold onto it. The gelatin should pop right out.

3 If using, place the fresh blackberries in the center opening of the unmolded gelatin. Serve immediately.

The Pineapple Upside Down

MAKES ONE 2-QUART (2 L) MOLD

For as long as I can remember, my mom would make a pineapple upside-down cake for me on my birthday. It was, and still is, my all-time favorite dessert. I believe that the love was passed down to me directly from my grandfather who also had this perfect dessert on his birthday. It has been great fun—and a bit of nostalgia—to take the flavors of this special cake and turn them into a gelatin mold that is just as delicious. There are three layers combining tart cherry, salty caramel, and sweet pineapple. When unmolded, the cherry layer will be the top layer followed by the salty caramel panna cotta layer, and on the bottom, the pineapple layer.

Vegetable oil for greasing the mold

CHERRY GELATIN

3 sheets gelatin, broken into small pieces

1 cup (237 ml) organic tart cherry juice

2 tablespoons sugar

2 teaspoons edible red glitter

SALTY CARAMEL PANNA COTTA

1 cup (200 g) sugar

¼ cup (59 ml) water, plus more for brushing down saucepan

Pinch of fine sea salt

3 cups (710 ml) heavy cream

1¾ cups (415 ml) whole milk

2 packets (7 g each) unflavored gelatin powder, such as Knox brand

PINEAPPLE GELATIN

4 cups (660 g) small cubes fresh pineapple

⅓ cup (67 g) sugar

Juice of 1 lime, strained of all pulp

8 sheets gelatin, broken into small pieces

Prepare the Mold

Lightly coat the interior of a 2-quart (2 L) mold with vegetable oil. Set aside.

(continued)

Make the Cherry Gelatin

1 Place the gelatin in a small saucepan. Add ½ cup (118 ml) of the cherry juice and set aside to bloom for 10 minutes. Then, add the sugar and the remaining juice and place over low heat. Heat, stirring frequently, until the gelatin has dissolved completely, about 4 minutes. Strain the liquid through a fine-mesh sieve into a small bowl. Transfer to the refrigerator until the gelatin has begun to thicken, about 20 minutes.

2 Remove the cherry gelatin from the refrigerator and add the glitter, stirring to distribute evenly. Pour the glittered cherry gelatin into the prepared mold and place the mold in the refrigerator. Refrigerate until just set, about 1 hour.

Make the Salty Caramel Panna Cotta

1 Place the sugar, water, and salt in a heavy-bottomed medium saucepan over medium-high heat. Cook, stirring gently once or twice until the sugar dissolves, then continue to cook, gently swirling the pan occasionally and washing down the sides of the pan with a pastry brush soaked in water as necessary to prevent crystals from forming, until it turns a deep caramel color, about 15 minutes. Caramelized sugar is extremely hot, so take care that it doesn't splash.

2 Meanwhile, place 1 cup (237 ml) of the cream in a small saucepan. Place over medium heat and bring to a simmer. Immediately remove from the heat. Whisking constantly, carefully and slowly pour the hot cream into the caramelized sugar. Be very, very careful as it will bubble up and can splatter. When completely blended, set aside to cool.

3 Place ¾ cup (177 ml) of the milk in a medium heatproof bowl. Sprinkle the gelatin over the milk and set aside to bloom for 10 minutes.

4 Place the remaining 1 cup (237 ml) of milk in a medium saucepan. Add the remaining 2 cups (473 ml) of cream and place over medium-high heat. Bring to a bare simmer and immediately remove from the heat. Quickly pour the hot milk mixture over the gelatin mixture, whisking vigorously until the gelatin has completely dissolved. Whisk in the caramel and set aside to cool to room temperature.

5 Remove the mold from the refrigerator. Strain the cooled caramel mixture through a fine-mesh sieve, then pour it over the set cherry layer and return to the refrigerator. Refrigerate until firm, about 3 hours.

Make the Pineapple Gelatin

1 Place the pineapple chunks in a medium saucepan. Add the sugar along with enough water to cover the fruit by a depth of 1 inch (2.5 cm). Place over medium-high heat and bring to a boil. Lower the heat and cook at a gentle simmer until the pineapple is very tender but not falling apart, about 45 minutes.

2 Strain the pineapple through a fine-mesh sieve into a large measuring cup to separate out the cooking liquid (set aside the pineapple solids in a medium bowl for later). Add the lime juice to the cooking liquid in the measuring cup. If you do not have 2 cups (473 ml) of liquid, add just enough cool water to make that amount. Set aside.

3 Place the gelatin pieces into a small saucepan. Add about ½ cup (118 ml) of the pineapple cooking liquid or just enough to generously cover. Set aside to bloom for 10 minutes. Add the remaining pineapple cooking liquid, then transfer to low heat and warm, stirring frequently, until the gelatin has dissolved completely, about 3 minutes. Strain the pineapple gelatin mixture through a fine-mesh sieve into a small bowl. Let come to room temperature.

Build the Layers

Remove the mold from the refrigerator and carefully spoon the reserved pineapple chunks over the panna cotta. Pour the pineapple gelatin on top. Tightly wrap the entire mold with plastic film. Transfer to the refrigerator until firm, about 3 hours or no more than 24 hours.

Unmold It

1 Remove the mold from the refrigerator. Remove and discard the plastic film. Place the mold in a bowl filled with hot water to come up to but not over the edge. Hold for 15 to 30 seconds to loosen. Watch carefully as you do not want the gelatin to begin melting.

2 Place a serving plate over the mold and invert the mold onto it. The gelatin should pop right out. Serve immediately, cut into slices.

Grandma's Ambrosia

MAKES ONE 6-CUP (1.4 L) MOLD

Ambrosia salad was a staple at all of our family events. Even today, the first bite takes me right back to my grandmother's kitchen where I used to sneak a taste while she was mixing all of the ingredients together. There is something about the combination of fruit and cream that is just so appealing, which is why I decided to leave her recipe pretty much just the way she always combined the fruits and flavors together.

Vegetable oil for greasing the mold

One 8-ounce (227 g) can crushed pineapple

1 packet (7 g) unflavored gelatin powder, such as Knox brand

One 15-ounce (425 g) can Coco López Cream of Coconut

2 cups (473 ml) strained fresh orange juice

1¾ cups (105 g) thawed Cool Whip

2 medium mandarin oranges, peeled and broken into segments, all pith removed

1½ cups (75 g) miniature marshmallows

½ cup (64 g) flaked coconut (optional)

½ cup (63 g) chopped toasted pecans (optional)

Prep the Mold

Lightly coat the interior of a 6-cup (1.4 L) mold with vegetable oil. Set aside.

Make the Gelatin

1 Place the pineapple in a fine-mesh sieve set over a small bowl. Allow all the liquid to drain off, then reserve the pineapple and liquid separately.

2 Transfer the pineapple liquid to a large measuring cup and add just enough cool water to equal 1 cup (237 ml). Place ½ cup (118 ml) of the pineapple liquid in a small saucepan. Sprinkle the gelatin over the top and set aside to bloom for 10 minutes.

3 Transfer the pan to low heat, add the cream of coconut along with the remaining ½ cup (118 ml) of pineapple liquid and cook, stirring frequently, until the gelatin has dissolved completely, about 4 minutes.

4 Remove the saucepan from the heat and stir in the orange juice. Transfer to a medium mixing bowl and place in the refrigerator until slightly thickened, about 1 hour.

5 Remove the mixture from the refrigerator. Add the Cool Whip and, using a wire whisk, beat until completely blended. Return the bowl to the refrigerator and let chill for 15 minutes.

6 Remove the mixture from the refrigerator and, using a rubber spatula, fold in the reserved pineapple along with the oranges and marshmallows and, if using, the coconut and pecans. Spoon the mixture into the prepared mold, gently smoothing the top. Tightly wrap the entire mold with plastic film. Transfer to the refrigerator until firm, about 5 hours or no more than 24 hours.

Unmold It

1 Remove the mold from the refrigerator. Remove and discard the plastic film. Place the mold in a bowl filled with hot water to come up to but not over the edge. Hold for 15 to 30 seconds to loosen. Watch carefully as you do not want the gelatin to begin melting.

2 Remove the mold from the water and wipe the exterior dry. Place a serving plate over the mold and invert the mold onto it. The gelatin should pop right out.

3 Serve immediately, cut into slices.

Panna Cotton Candy

MAKES SIX 6-OUNCE (177 ML) DESSERT CUPS

This recipe was definitely inspired by my mom's love of cotton candy. I can always tell when she spots someone selling it because her eyes light up and she immediately gets this childlike smile on her face. I have done my best to mimic the exact flavor of cotton candy and the angled, two-toned palette of the finished dish adds a bit of circus-like fun. You do have to think a bit ahead to make it as, unless you have the big top in town, you have to order the cotton candy and the flavoring online. You need the real thing for the delicate texture and the flavoring to create the exact nostalgic taste that all kids (and some moms) love. If you are not planning to unmold the gelatins, use glass containers so that the angled layers can be seen.

Vegetable oil for greasing the molds

PINK COTTON CANDY GELATIN

2 cups (473 ml) heavy cream

1 packet (7 g) unflavored gelatin powder, such as Knox brand

2 ounces (57 g) pink cotton candy (see Notes)

15 drops food-grade cotton candy flavoring, such as LorAnn Oils (see Notes)

BLUE COTTON CANDY GELATIN

2 cups (473 ml) heavy cream

1 packet (7 g) packet unflavored gelatin powder, such as Knox brand

2 ounces (57 g) blue cotton candy (see Notes)

15 drops food-grade cotton candy flavoring, such as LorAnn Oils (see Notes)

Sprinkles for garnish (see Notes)

Prep the Molds

Lightly coat the interior of six 6-ounce (177 ml) dessert cups or glasses with vegetable oil. Set aside.

(continued)

Make the Pink Cotton Candy Gelatin

1 Place 1 cup (237 ml) of the cream in a medium saucepan. Sprinkle the gelatin over the top and set aside to bloom for 10 minutes.

2 Transfer the pan to low heat, add the remaining 1 cup (237 ml) of cream, and heat, stirring frequently, until the gelatin has dissolved completely, about 4 minutes.

3 Remove the pan from the heat and immediately add the pink cotton candy, stirring until the cotton candy has dissolved completely. Add the cotton candy flavoring, stirring to incorporate completely. Pour an equal portion of the pink cotton candy mixture into each of the prepared dessert cups, filling about halfway.

4 Fold a dish towel into quarters and place it on a refrigerator shelf. Transfer the cups to the refrigerator, placing one edge of each cup on the towel so that they sit at a slight angle. This will allow the gelatin to then set at that angle. Let chill until firm, about 1 hour.

Make the Blue Cotton Candy Gelatin

1 Place 1 cup (237 ml) of the cream in a medium saucepan. Sprinkle the packet of gelatin over the top and set aside to bloom for 10 minutes.

2 Transfer the saucepan to low heat, add the remaining 1 cup (237 ml) of cream, and heat, stirring frequently, until the gelatin has dissolved completely, about 4 minutes.

3 Remove the pan from the heat and immediately add the blue cotton candy, stirring until the cotton candy has dissolved completely. Add the cotton candy flavoring, stirring to incorporate completely. Set aside to cool to room temperature.

Build the Layers

1 Remove the dessert cups and the dish towel (you will no longer need it) from the refrigerator. Pour an equal portion of the blue cotton candy mixture over the firm pink cotton candy gelatin in each of the dessert cups.

2 Tightly cover each cup with plastic film and return it to the refrigerator. Chill until firm, about 3 hours.

Unmold Them

1 Remove the dessert cups from the refrigerator. Remove and discard the plastic film. Working with one at a time, place a dessert cup in a bowl filled with hot water to come up to but not over the edge. Hold for 15 to 30 seconds to loosen. Watch carefully as you do not want the water to come over the edge of the cup or the gelatin to begin melting. Remove the cup from the water and wipe the exterior dry.

2 Place a dessert plate over the dessert cup and invert the cup onto it. The gelatin should pop right out. If using the optional sprinkles, gently scatter them around the plate and over the top of each dessert. Do this immediately before serving as the sprinkles will quickly begin to melt. Repeat with the remaining cups and sprinkles.

3 Serve immediately.

Notes Cotton candy is available from specialty candy stores or online. I use the Just Hangin' brand, which I found on Amazon. Cotton candy flavoring is available online from www.lorannoils.com.

For these cups, I use Purple Pony Party Sprinkles, which are a combination of bright pinks, blues, and purples in a variety of shapes and sizes. They are available online from unitedbakerysupplies.com. If you can't find them, feel free to use any sprinkles you wish.

Honeydew Raz

MAKES ONE 6-CUP (1.4 L) MOLD

Honeydew melon is so underrepresented in desserts. For this recipe, I paired the cool refreshing flavor of honeydew with the bright, tart bite of raspberry for a perfect summertime showstopper! Add the gilded raspberries as a garnish, and you will have an awesome presentation. When unmolded, the honeydew layer will be the top layer with the raspberry layer on the bottom. Due to the weight of the ingredients in the creamy honeydew layer, you may notice what looks like an extra layer in the middle. Fear not, this is normal and will not compromise the beautiful flavor.

Vegetable oil for greasing the mold

CREAMY HONEYDEW GELATIN

2 cups (473 ml) heavy cream

2 packets (7 g each) unflavored gelatin powder, such as Knox brand

1½ cups (300 g) sugar

1 large (19 ounces/540 g) very ripe honeydew melon, peeled, seeded, and chopped

Juice of 1 lemon

RASPBERRY GELATIN

1 cup (237 ml) water

2 tablespoons sugar

2 containers (6 ounces/170 g each) fresh raspberries

Juice of 1 lemon, strained

1 packet (7 g) unflavored gelatin powder, such as Knox brand

1 teaspoon edible gold glitter

1 teaspoon edible pink glitter (optional)

12 to 16 raspberries (optional)

Prep the Mold

Lightly coat the interior of a 6-cup (1.4 L) mold with vegetable oil. Set aside.

Make the Creamy Honeydew Gelatin

1 Place the cream in a small saucepan. Sprinkle the gelatin over the top and set aside to bloom for 10 minutes.

(continued)

2 Add the sugar to the cream and place the pan over medium heat. Cook, stirring frequently, until the sugar has dissolved and the mixture is smooth and lump-free, about 5 minutes.

3 Place the chopped melon and lemon juice in the bowl of a food processor fitted with the metal blade. Process on high until very smooth. Add the hot cream mixture and process to blend completely.

4 Remove the bowl from the processor and, using a fine-mesh sieve, strain the mixture into the prepared mold. Discard the solids. Transfer to the refrigerator and let set until firm, at least 3 hours.

Make the Raspberry Gelatin

1 Combine the water and sugar in a medium saucepan over medium heat. Cook, stirring frequently, until the sugar has dissolved, about 4 minutes. Stir in the raspberries and bring to a boil. Immediately lower the heat and cook, stirring occasionally, until the raspberries are mashed into the liquid, about 5 minutes.

2 Remove the pan from the heat and strain the mixture through a fine-mesh sieve into a medium heatproof bowl. Discard the solids.

3 Stir in the lemon juice and then measure the liquid. You will need exactly 2 cups (473 ml). If you have too much, discard the extra; if too little, add enough cool water to make the desired 2 cups (473 ml). Return the liquid to the saucepan. Sprinkle the gelatin over the liquid and set aside to bloom for 10 minutes.

4 Place the raspberry mixture over low heat and cook, stirring occasionally, until the gelatin has dissolved, about 5 minutes.

Build the Layers

1 Pour the raspberry mixture through a fine-mesh sieve into a clean small bowl and transfer to the refrigerator until it just begins to thicken, about 20 minutes. Add the gold edible glitter, stirring to distribute evenly.

2 Carefully spoon the thickened, glittered raspberry gelatin over the set honeydew layer. Wrap the entire mold in plastic film and return to the refrigerator and let set for 8 hours or up to 24 hours.

Unmold It

1 Remove the mold from the refrigerator. Remove and discard the plastic film. Place the mold in a bowl filled with hot water to come up to but not over the edge. Hold for 15 to 30 seconds to loosen. Watch carefully as you do not want the gelatin to begin melting.

2 Remove the mold from the water and wipe the exterior dry. Place a serving plate over the mold and invert the mold onto it. The gelatin should pop right out.

3 If using, place the edible pink glitter in a small resealable plastic bag. Add the 12 to 16 raspberries and gently shake to coat each raspberry. Carefully place the individual glittery raspberries on top of the honeydew gelatin.

4 Serve immediately.

Deconstructed Colada

MAKES ONE 7-CUP (1.7 L) MOLD

This very sweet but deliciously tropical dessert will transport you to vacation, sipping coladas by the pool. Got a case of the winter blues? Whip this up and you will immediately be lounging in a hammock, relaxed and carefree. When unmolded, the pineapple gelatin will be the top layer followed by the coconut cream gelatin.

Vegetable oil for greasing the molds

PINEAPPLE GELATIN

4 cups (680 g) small cubes fresh pineapple

⅓ cup (67 g) sugar

½ cup (95 g) maraschino cherries, well drained

Juice of 1 lime, strained of all pulp

5 sheets gelatin, broken into pieces

COCONUT CREAM GELATIN

1 tablespoon unflavored gelatin powder, such as Knox brand

3 tablespoons (45 ml) cool water

1 can (15 ounces/425 g) Coco López Cream of Coconut

1 can (13.5 ounces/400 ml) unsweetened coconut milk

2 cups (473 ml) heavy cream, chilled

¼ cup (32 g) confectioners' sugar

Prep the Mold

Lightly coat the interior of a 7-cup (1.7 L) mold with vegetable oil. Set aside.

Make the Pineapple Gelatin

1 Place the pineapple in a medium saucepan. Add the sugar along with enough water to cover the fruit by a depth of 1 inch (2.5 cm). Place over medium-high heat and bring to a boil. Lower the heat and cook at a gentle simmer until the pineapple is very tender, but not falling apart, about 45 minutes.

2 Strain the pineapple through a fine-mesh sieve into a large measuring cup, separating the fruit and the juice. Spoon 1 cup (170 g) of the pineapple into a medium mixing bowl (reserve the remaining pineapple for another use). Add the cherries to pineapple in the bowl, stirring to combine. Set aside.

3 Add the lime juice to the strained pineapple cooking liquid in the measuring cup. You will need exactly 2 cups (473 ml) of liquid. If you have too much, discard the extra; if too little, add just enough cold water to make the desired 2 cups (473 ml). Set aside.

4 Place the gelatin pieces in a small saucepan. Add about ¼ cup (59 ml) of the strained pineapple liquid or just enough to generously cover the gelatin pieces. Set aside to bloom for about 10 minutes. Then add the remaining pineapple liquid and transfer to low heat. Warm, stirring frequently, until the gelatin has dissolved completely, about 3 minutes. Strain the liquid through a fine-mesh sieve into a small bowl. Set aside to come to room temperature.

Build the Layers

1 Pour about one-third (5⅓ ounces/158 ml) of the pineapple-lime liquid into the prepared mold. Transfer to the freezer and allow to chill until just beginning to firm, about 15 minutes. Do not allow the liquid to freeze as it will alter the consistency and you will have to start from scratch.

2 Remove the mold from the freezer and carefully spoon the pineapple-cherry mixture over the barely set gelatin. Pour another third (5⅓ ounces/158 ml) of the pineapple-lime liquid over the top and transfer to the refrigerator. Refrigerate until firm, about 3 hours.

3 Remove the mold from the refrigerator and spoon on the remaining pineapple-lime liquid. Return to the refrigerator and let set until firm, for 3 hours.

Make the Coconut Cream Gelatin

1 Place the gelatin in a small bowl. Add the cool water and set aside to bloom for about 10 minutes.

2 Prepare an ice-water bath in a large bowl (see box, page 127). Set aside.

(continued)

3 Combine the cream of coconut and the coconut milk in a medium saucepan over medium heat. Bring to a bare simmer. Lower the heat and whisk in the bloomed gelatin, whisking to ensure that the gelatin has dissolved into the coconut liquid.

4 Remove the coconut mixture from the heat and pour it through a fine-mesh sieve into a medium bowl (it should easily fit into the large bowl of ice water). Set the coconut mixture into the ice-water bath, taking care that the water does not come up and over the edge. Using a rubber spatula, gently and occasionally stir the coconut mixture until it begins to thicken, about 15 minutes.

5 Meanwhile, combine the heavy cream and confectioners' sugar, whisking to dissolve the sugar.

6 When the coconut mixture has begun to set, immediately remove it from the ice-water bath. Stir the heavy cream mixture into the coconut mixture, mixing gently to completely blend.

Build the Layers

Remove the mold from the refrigerator. Spoon the coconut mixture over the top of the pineapple-cherry gelatin, smoothing to an even layer. Wrap the entire mold in plastic film and return to the refrigerator and let set for at least 4 hours or up to 24 hours.

Unmold It

1 Remove the mold from the refrigerator. Remove and discard the plastic film. Place the mold in a bowl filled with hot water to come up to but not over the edge. Hold for 15 to 30 seconds to loosen. Watch carefully as you do not want the gelatin to begin melting.

2 Place a serving plate over the mold and invert the mold onto it. The gelatin should pop right out. Serve immediately.

Brigadeiro Surprise

MAKES FOUR 5-OUNCE (147 ML) DESSERT CUPS OR METAL MOLDS

On a recent trip to Brazil I could not get enough of one of their signature sweets, the brigadeiro, a rich chocolate fudge ball. If you have never tried one, now is the time to indulge. Here these sugar bombs are hidden inside a beautiful vanilla bean panna cotta.

You can use any 5- to 6-ounce (147 to 177 ml) molds for these, but they are especially interesting when made in one of the ornate decorative metal molds popular in the 1940s and '50s. The bridadeiro recipe makes more fudge balls than needed for the gelatin molds. They are so delicious, I always keep extras on hand to satisfy my sweet tooth.

Vegetable oil for greasing the molds

2 cups (473 ml) heavy cream

1 packet (7 g) unflavored gelatin powder, such as Knox brand

½ cup (100 g) sugar

½ vanilla bean, split lengthwise

4 brigadeiros, homemade (recipe follows) or store-bought

Prep the Molds

Lightly coat the interior of each of the dessert cups or molds with vegetable oil. Set aside.

Make the Panna Cotta

1 Place 1 cup (237 ml) of the cream in a small saucepan. Sprinkle the gelatin over the top and set aside to bloom for 10 minutes.

2 Add the remaining 1 cup (237 ml) of cream along with the sugar to the mixture in the saucepan. Scrape in the vanilla seeds and then add the bean pod. Place over low heat and heat, stirring constantly, until the sugar and gelatin have dissolved, about 4 minutes. Continue to cook, stirring frequently, until well flavored with vanilla, another 10 minutes.

(continued)

3 Remove from the heat and pour through a fine-mesh sieve into a medium mixing bowl. Refrigerate, stirring occasionally, until chilled, about 30 minutes.

4 Carefully spoon the chilled cream mixture halfway into each of the prepared molds (reserve the rest). Refrigerate until completely set, about 30 minutes.

Build the Layers

1 Remove the panna cottas from the refrigerator and place a brigadeiro in the center of each. Spoon enough of the reserved cream mixture over each brigadeiro to completely cover. As you spoon, it might be necessary to hold the brigadeiro down so that it stays firmly in the center.

2 Wrap each cup in plastic film and return to the refrigerator until completely set, at least 2 hours or no more than 8 hours.

Unmold Them

1 Remove and discard the plastic film. Working with one at a time, place a dessert cup in a bowl filled with hot water to come up to but not over the edge. Hold for 15 to 30 seconds to loosen. Watch carefully as you do not want the water to come over the edge of the cup or the gelatin to begin melting. Remove the cup from the water and wipe the exterior dry. Place a small dessert plate over the cup and invert the cup onto it. The panna cotta should pop right out.

2 Serve immediately.

Brigadeiros

MAKES 20 CHOCOLATES

Softened butter for greasing a plate and your hands

Chocolate sprinkles or any other sprinkle you prefer

1 can (14 ounces/397 g) sweetened condensed milk

3 tablespoons (22 g) unsweetened cocoa powder, sifted

1 tablespoon unsalted butter

Pinch of sea salt

1 Lightly coat a flat plate with butter. Lay a piece of parchment paper on a second plate and the sprinkles on a third. This will be your brigadeiro assembly line. Set aside.

2 Combine the condensed milk, cocoa powder, unsalted butter, and salt in a medium saucepan. Set over medium heat and cook, stirring constantly with a silicone spatula, until the mixture thickens and you can run the spatula through the middle without it immediately (within 2 to 3 seconds) flowing back together, about 12 minutes. Scrape the chocolate mixture onto the buttered plate and refrigerate until well chilled and firm, about 1 hour.

3 Remove the chocolate mixture from the refrigerator. Lightly coat your hands with softened butter and scoop up about a tablespoon of the chocolate mixture. Place it in the palm of your hand and roll it back and forth to form a smooth, round ball. Transfer the ball to the plate of sprinkles and gently roll it around to cover all over. Place each finished brigadeiro on the parchment paper–lined plate. The brigadeiros will keep, covered and refrigerated, for up to 5 days.

Lemony Blueberry Layers

MAKES FOUR 8-OUNCE (237 ML) GLASSES

This very lemony dessert is my take on the very delicious traditional lemon bar cookie. I have added chopped blueberries for their wonderful color as well as for the way they seem to marry so well with the deep lemon essence—try slicing them over a bowl so you don't lose their juice. I know that the zest of 5 lemons seems like a lot, but it really does make an intensely flavored cream layer. Plus, you can use the zested lemons to make a big pitcher of lemonade (or Lemonade Jiggler, page 22). You'll need glass dessert cups for this.

BLUEBERRY GELATIN

2 cups (340 grams) chopped fresh blueberries

1½ cups (355 ml) water

¼ cup (50 g) sugar

1 tablespoon fresh lemon juice

1 packet (7 g) unflavored gelatin powder, such as Knox brand

¼ teaspoon edible silver glitter

LEMON CREAM GELATIN

2 cups (473 ml) heavy cream

Zest of 5 organic lemons

½ vanilla bean, split lengthwise

1 packet (7 g) unflavored gelatin powder, such as Knox brand

½ cup (100 g) sugar

GARNISH (OPTIONAL)

4 strips lemon peel

20 whole blueberries

Edible silver glitter

Make the Blueberry Gelatin

1 Combine the chopped blueberries with the water, sugar, and lemon juice in a small saucepan over medium heat. Cook, stirring frequently, until the sugar has dissolved and the blueberries are mushy, about 12 minutes.

(continued)

2 Remove from the heat and sprinkle the gelatin over the top. Set aside to bloom for 10 minutes.

3 Return the blueberry mixture to low heat and cook, stirring constantly, until the gelatin has dissolved completely, about 4 minutes. Remove from the heat and pour through a fine-mesh sieve into a large shallow bowl. Discard the solids. Place in the freezer until just beginning to thicken, about 30 minutes.

4 Remove from the freezer and stir in the glitter so it's suspended throughout. (If not, return the gelatin to the freezer for another 15 minutes and stir again.) Spoon ¼ cup (57 g) of the mixture into each of four 8-ounce (237 ml) glasses (reserve the remaining blueberry mixture in the refrigerator). Refrigerate the quarter-filled glasses until set completely, about 1 hour.

Make the Lemon Cream Gelatin

1 Place the cream and lemon zest in a medium saucepan. Scrape the seeds from the vanilla bean into the cream, add the scraped bean pod, place over medium-low heat, and cook, stirring frequently, until very warm and aromatic, 5 minutes. Remove from the heat and set aside to steep for 30 minutes.

2 Strain the lemon cream mixture through a fine-mesh sieve into a clean medium saucepan. Sprinkle the gelatin over the top and set aside to bloom for 10 minutes.

3 Add the sugar to the lemon cream mixture, place over medium heat, and bring to a boil. Lower the heat to a bare simmer and continue to cook, stirring, until the gelatin and sugar have dissolved, about 3 minutes. Remove the lemon cream mixture from the heat and strain it again through a fine-mesh sieve into a large shallow bowl. Place in the freezer and chill, stirring occasionally, until just beginning to thicken, about 30 minutes.

Build the Layers and Garnish

1 Remove the blueberry-filled glasses from the refrigerator. Spoon about ¼ cup (57 g) of the lemon cream gelatin into each one. Transfer to the freezer to chill until completely set, about 20 minutes.

2 Repeat the layering and chilling process as above, adding ¼ cup (57 g) of the reserved blueberry gelatin to form the third layer, letting it set in the freezer for 20 minutes, and then adding ¼ cup (57 g) of the lemon cream gelatin to form the fourth and final layer, and letting it set in the freezer for a final 20 minutes. Each dessert will have 4 alternating layers.

3 When ready to serve, garnish each dessert glass with a strip of lemon peel, a few blueberries, and a sprinkle of glitter, if desired.

Dark Choco Orange

MAKES ONE 1-QUART (1 L) MOLD

I've always loved chocolate-covered candied orange peel. The slight bitterness of the dark chocolate combined with the acidic yet sweet candied peel makes a perfect marriage. For this recipe, I tried to take the two flavors of the candy and marry them in the exact same way. The sea salt garnish just seems to bring the flavors all together.

Vegetable oil for greasing the mold

4½ cups (1.1 L) heavy cream

2 packets (7 g each) unflavored gelatin powder, such as Knox brand

Zest of 1 orange

½ cup (100 g) sugar

½ teaspoon Grand Marnier

9 ounces (254 g) 70% dark chocolate, chopped into small pieces

Candied orange peel for garnish (see Note)

Sea salt flakes for garnish

Prep the Mold

Lightly coat the interior of a 1-quart (1 L) mold with vegetable oil. Set aside.

Make the Gelatin

1 Place ½ cup (118 ml) of the cream into a small bowl. Sprinkle the gelatin over the top and set aside to bloom for 10 minutes.

2 Place the remaining cream in a small saucepan. Add the orange zest along with the sugar and Grand Marnier and place over low heat. Cook, stirring constantly, until the sugar has dissolved and the mixture is smooth, about 5 minutes. Add the chocolate and continue to cook, whisking constantly, until the chocolate has melted and the mixture is smooth and glossy, about 5 minutes. Add the reserved gelatin mixture and continue to cook, whisking constantly, until the gelatin has dissolved and is incorporated completely, about 4 minutes.

3 Remove from the heat and pour the mixture through a fine-mesh sieve into the prepared mold. Wrap the entire mold in plastic film and refrigerate until completely set, 3 hours or up to 24 hours.

Unmold It

1 Remove and discard the plastic film. Place the mold in a large bowl filled with hot water to come up to but not over the edge. Hold for 15 seconds to loosen. Watch carefully as you do not want the water to come up over the edge of the mold or the gelatin to begin melting. Remove the mold from the water and wipe the exterior dry. Place a serving plate over the mold and invert the mold onto it. The gelatin should pop right out.

2 If using, arrange the candied orange peel randomly over the top and sprinkle with sea salt flakes.

3 Serve immediately.

Note Candied orange peel is available at many supermarkets and specialty food stores, confectionery shops, or online.

Orange Cream Terrazzo Dream

MAKES ONE 6-CUP (1.4 L) MOLD

The combination of orange and vanilla immediately takes me back to family vacations at the Jersey Shore. To me, the orange and vanilla soft-serve twists I ate there are still an unmatched pairing. I've upgraded that flavor profile a bit by combining two types of Sanpellegrino orange drinks—traditional orange and blood orange—with pure vanilla. I also turned to my background in design and one of my favorite materials, terrazzo, to make this throwback dessert a visual showstopper. When sliced, the two-toned orange cubes make a beautiful terrazzo-like design in the vanilla-flavored gelatin.

Vegetable oil for greasing the baking dish and mold

BLOOD ORANGE GELATIN

2 cups (473 ml) Sanpellegrino Aranciata Rossa (see Note)

1 packet (7 g) unflavored gelatin powder, such as Knox brand

1 tablespoon sugar

ORANGE GELATIN

2 cups (473 ml) Sanpellegrino Aranciata (see Note)

1 packet (7 g) unflavored gelatin powder, such as Knox brand

1 tablespoon sugar

VANILLA GELATIN

¼ cup (59 ml) water

1 packet (7 g) unflavored gelatin powder, such as Knox brand

2 cups (473 ml) whole milk

2 tablespoons sugar

1 tablespoon pure vanilla extract

½ vanilla bean, split lengthwise

Prep the Molds

Lightly coat an 11 × 7-inch (28 × 17 cm) baking dish and a 6-cup (1.4 L) mold with vegetable oil. Set aside.

(continued)

Make the Blood Orange Gelatin

1 Place 1 cup (237 ml) of the Aranciata Rossa in a medium saucepan. Sprinkle the gelatin over the top and set aside to bloom for 10 minutes.

2 Add the remaining 1 cup (237 ml) of Aranciata Rossa along with the sugar to the bloomed gelatin and place over low heat. Cook, stirring constantly, until the gelatin has dissolved completely, about 4 minutes. Remove the pan from the heat and pour through a fine-mesh sieve into the prepared baking dish. Refrigerate until completely set, about 1 hour.

3 Remove the dish from the refrigerator and, using a small sharp knife, roughly chop the gelatin into ½-inch cubes (1.27 cm). The pieces do not have to be perfect. Place them in a medium bowl and refrigerate.

4 Wipe the baking dish clean and again lightly coat it with vegetable oil. Set aside.

Make the Orange Gelatin

1 Place 1 cup (237 ml) of the Aranciata in a medium saucepan. Sprinkle the gelatin over the top and set aside to bloom for 10 minutes.

2 Add the remaining 1 cup (237 ml) of Aranciata along with the sugar to the bloomed gelatin and place over low heat. Cook, stirring constantly, until the gelatin has dissolved completely, about 4 minutes. Remove the pan from the heat and pour the mixture through a fine-mesh sieve into the prepared baking dish. Refrigerate until completely set, about 1 hour.

3 Remove the dish from the refrigerator and, using a small sharp knife, roughly chop the gelatin into ½-inch (1.27 cm) cubes. The pieces do not have to be perfect. Place them in a medium bowl and refrigerate.

Make the Vanilla Gelatin

1 Place the water in a medium saucepan. Sprinkle the gelatin over the top and set aside to bloom for 10 minutes.

2 Add the milk, sugar, and vanilla extract to the bloomed gelatin. Using a small, sharp knife, scrape the vanilla seeds into the mixture. Add the scraped bean pod and place over medium heat. Cook, stirring, until the gelatin has dissolved completely, about 4 minutes.

3 Bring to a gentle simmer and cook, stirring occasionally, until well flavored with vanilla, about 10 minutes. Remove the pan from the heat and pour the mixture through a fine-mesh sieve into a bowl. Set aside to come to room temperature.

Build the Layers

1 Place a mixture of the two types of orange-flavored cubes into the bottom of the prepared mold, coming up about one-third of the way. Add enough of the vanilla mixture to completely cover the orange cubes. Refrigerate until completely set, about 1 hour. Return the reserved gelatin cubes to the refrigerator until ready to make the next layer.

2 Continue making layers until all the cubes and vanilla mixture have been used, ending with the vanilla, allowing each layer to set before proceeding with the following layer. Tightly wrap the entire mold with plastic film. Return to the refrigerator and let set for 8 hours or up to 24 hours.

Unmold It

1 Remove and discard the plastic film. Place the mold in a large bowl filled with hot water to come up to but not over the edge. Hold for 15 seconds, taking care that the gelatin does not begin melting. Remove the mold from the water and wipe the exterior dry. Place a serving plate over the mold and invert the mold onto it. The gelatin should pop right out.

2 Serve immediately, cut into slices.

Note Sanpellegrino drinks are widely available at most major supermarkets and big-box retailers, such as Target, as well as online.

Banoffee Bombs

MAKES SIX 3-INCH (7.62 CM) SEMISPHERICAL DOME MOLDS

Once I tasted the classic English dessert called banoffee tart, I was addicted. When I started playing with gelatin, I just had to create my own take on it using a marvelous small semispherical silicone mold form that can be ordered online (see Sources, page 163). The dome shape and the crackling bottom layer of chocolate turn this into something sensational on the plate.

Vegetable oil for greasing the molds

2 cups (473 ml) heavy cream

½ cup (100 g) sugar

2 large egg whites

5 ripe but firm bananas, peeled and cut into pieces

1 cup (237 ml) whole milk

1 teaspoon pure vanilla extract

½ teaspoon ground cinnamon

2 packets (7 g each) unflavored gelatin powder, such as Knox brand

1 can (15 ounces/425 g) dulce de leche

Chocolate hard shell, such as Smucker's Magic Shell

Prep the Molds

Lightly coat the interior of each of six 3-inch (7.62 cm) silicone semi-spherical dome mold cups with vegetable oil. Set aside.

Make the Banana Cream Gelatin

1 Place the heavy cream along with ¼ cup (50 g) of the sugar in a medium mixing bowl. Using a handheld electric mixer, beat until firm peaks form, about 6 minutes. Set aside.

2 Place the egg whites with the remaining ¼ cup (50 g) of sugar in a medium mixing bowl. Using a handheld electric mixer, beat until firm peaks form, about 5 minutes. Scoop the beaten egg whites into the whipped cream, using a rubber spatula to gently fold them together until completely blended. Transfer to the refrigerator.

3 Combine the bananas, ½ cup (118 ml) of the milk, vanilla, and cinnamon in the bowl of a food processor fitted with the metal blade. Process to a smooth puree. Place a fine-mesh sieve over a medium mixing bowl. Scrape the banana mixture from the processor bowl into the sieve, pressing gently to push the mixture through, discarding any solids left behind. Rinse and dry the sieve as you will need it again.

4 Place the remaining ½ cup (118 ml) of milk in a small saucepan. Sprinkle the gelatin over the top and set aside to bloom for 15 minutes.

5 Transfer the bloomed gelatin to low heat and cook, stirring occasionally, until the gelatin has dissolved completely, about 4 minutes. Remove from the heat and pour through a fine-mesh sieve into the banana puree. Stir to combine completely.

6 Remove the whipped cream mixture from the refrigerator and gently fold it into the banana puree until completely blended. Spoon the mixture into the prepared silicone half spheres, filling about three-quarters full. Using a rubber spatula, gently smooth the tops. Refrigerate until firm to the touch, about 1 hour.

Fill and Coat the Bombs

1 Remove the bombs from the refrigerator. Using a teaspoon, scoop out a round hole in the center of each, leaving about a ½-inch (1.27 cm) edge of banana cream around the cavity. Working with one at a time, carefully spoon enough of the dulce de leche into the cavity to fill completely. Transfer the molds to the freezer and let chill until beginning to firm, about 30 minutes.

2 Remove from the freezer and wrap the entire mold form in plastic film. Return to the freezer until the cream is completely set, about 1 hour.

3 Remove and discard the plastic film. Spoon the chocolate hard shell over the flat side of each bomb. Return to the freezer and let set, uncovered, for another 3 hours.

Unmold Them

1 Working with one at time, gently push on the silicone until the gelatin releases (because it is frozen, it should pop right out into your hand). Quickly transfer the bombs, rounded side up, to a dessert plate.

2 Serve immediately.

Gimme S'more Wiggle

MAKES 4 TO 6 COUPE GLASSES

So many of my childhood memories include telling ghost stories and getting messy making s'mores around a campfire. This jiggle dish has all of the elements and flavors of the classic campfire treat: graham crackers, chocolate, and toasty marshmallows. One bite of this dessert takes me right back to that time. I hope it does the same for you.

I like to make these in champagne coupe glasses but you can use any 6- to 8-ounce (177 to 237 ml) mold, or even a single large 6-cup (1.4 L) mold. If you have a kitchen torch, use it to toast the marshmallow on top. It adds the perfect touch to the finished dessert.

GRAHAM CRACKER CREAM GELATIN

2 cups (473 ml) heavy cream

8 graham cracker squares, broken into pieces

1 packet (7 g) unflavored gelatin powder, such as Knox brand

CHOCOLATE GELATIN

2 cups (473 ml) heavy cream

1 packet (7 g) unflavored gelatin powder, such as Knox brand

¼ cup (50 g) sugar

4½ ounces (127 g) 70% dark chocolate, chopped

TOPPING

6 large marshmallows

2 graham crackers, crumbled (optional)

Edible gold glitter (optional)

Make the Graham Cracker Cream Gelatin

1 Place the heavy cream in a medium saucepan. Add the graham cracker pieces and place over medium heat. Bring to a simmer, lower the heat, and cook at a gentle simmer, stirring frequently, for 15 minutes. Remove from the heat and let infuse for 15 minutes.

2 Pour the cream through a fine-mesh sieve into a clean small saucepan. Sprinkle the gelatin over the top and set aside to bloom for 10 minutes.

(continued)

3 Place the saucepan over low heat and cook, stirring constantly, until the gelatin has dissolved completely, about 10 minutes. Pour through a fine-mesh sieve into a clean bowl. Let cool to room temperature.

4 When cooled, fill each of six coupe glasses about halfway full with the graham cracker gelatin. Refrigerate until beginning to thicken, about 30 minutes.

Make the Chocolate Gelatin

1 Place 1 cup (237 ml) of the cream in a medium saucepan. Sprinkle the gelatin over the top and set aside to bloom for 10 minutes.

2 Add the remaining 1 cup (237 ml) of cream along with the sugar and chocolate. Place over low heat and cook, stirring constantly, until the sugar has dissolved completely and the chocolate has melted. Pour the mixture through a fine-mesh sieve into a clean bowl. Refrigerate until beginning to thicken, about 30 minutes.

Build the Layers and Top

1 Remove the glasses from the refrigerator and carefully pour an equal portion of the chocolate mixture over the cream layer. Refrigerate until thick enough to hold a marshmallow upright, about 30 minutes.

2 Remove from the refrigerator and place a large marshmallow in the center of each gelatin, either upright or at a slight angle. Tightly cover each glass with plastic film and return it to the refrigerator. Chill until completely set, about 2 hours or no more than 8 hours.

3 Remove and discard the plastic film. If using the kitchen torch, ignite it and lightly toast each marshmallow by holding the torch about 1 inch (2.5 cm) away while gently moving it around all sides until the marshmallow is light brown and bubbling.

4 If desired, sprinkle graham cracker crumbles around the edge of the marshmallow and toss on a few touches of gold glitter. Serve immediately.

Chapter 3

Savory Dishes

Savory Aspic

MAKES ABOUT 3¼ CUPS (769 ML)

This is a simple aspic that can be used to hold together a terrine or any other savory recipe requiring a clear gelatin. The gelatin will be tinted by the type of broth used; a clear homemade, defatted chicken stock will result in the cleanest, clearest look. On its own it makes a lovely summer chilled soup, particularly when you add barely cooked diced vegetables, such as carrots, summer squashes, or turnips or tiny peas.

2 packets (7 g each) unflavored gelatin powder, such as Knox brand

¼ cup (59 ml) cold water

3 cups (710 ml) hot, low-sodium, fat-free chicken, beef, or vegetable broth

Salt to taste

¼ cup (59 ml) dry Madeira or marsala wine

Make the Savory Gelatin

Combine the gelatin with the cold water in a medium bowl. Set aside to bloom for 10 minutes. Stir in ¼ cup (59 ml) of the hot broth and season with salt. Stir to completely dissolve the gelatin. Add the remaining hot broth along with the wine. (From this point, you can use it in another recipe as directed.)

Serve as a Chilled Soup

1 Pour through a fine-mesh sieve into whatever container you are using and tightly cover the entire container with plastic film. Refrigerate to chill for at least 3 hours or up to 24 hours.

2 Remove and discard the plastic film. Using a fork, break the gelatin into small chunks. Spoon an equal portion of the chunks into each of eight consommé bowls. Garnish with a sprinkling of fresh herbs, a touch of sour cream, or any vegetable dice that appeals to you.

3 Serve immediately.

Simple Jellied Consommé Madrilene

MAKES 4 CUPS (1 L)

This is an old-fashioned soup, most often served at very fancy restaurant dinners in the early part of the last century. In those days, making the stock or broth was a labor-intensive, hours-long experience where the addition of bones and hoofs created not only the broth but the gelatin. This is a light, delicious soup that, in small soup cups, makes a marvelous first course or in a larger shallow soup bowl makes a light lunch. I like to garnish it with poached shrimp, crabmeat, or diced chicken for a more substantial lunch.

½ cup (118 ml) cool water

2 packets (7 g each) unflavored gelatin powder, such as Knox brand

2 cups (473 ml) tomato juice

2 cups (473 ml) low-sodium chicken broth

½ cup (26 g) finely diced onion

¼ cup (13 g) finely diced celery, plus chopped celery leaves for garnish

1 tablespoon strained fresh lemon juice

2 sprigs fresh thyme

1 teaspoon dried marjoram

½ teaspoon paprika

Salt and white pepper

8 lemon slices for garnish

Make the Gelatin

1 Place the cool water in a small bowl. Sprinkle the gelatin over the top and set aside to bloom for 10 minutes.

2 Combine the tomato juice and chicken broth in a medium saucepan. Add the onion, celery, lemon juice, thyme, marjoram, and paprika. Season with salt and white pepper and place over medium heat. Bring to a boil and boil until the liquid is infused with the flavor of the vegetables and herbs, 4 minutes.

(continued)

3 Remove the pan from the heat and add the reserved gelatin mixture, stirring to blend completely. Strain through a fine-mesh sieve into a medium mixing bowl. Tightly cover the entire bowl with plastic film. Refrigerate until completely set, about 4 hours or no more than 24 hours.

Unmold and Serve

1 When ready to serve, remove and discard the plastic film. Using a fork, break the gelatin into small chunks. Divide them equally among eight consommé bowls. Garnish with a sprinkling of the chopped celery leaves and a lemon slice.

2 Serve immediately.

Goats 'n' Beets Bites

MAKES ABOUT 22 BITE-SIZE GELATINS

This gelatin combination reflects the flavors of the very popular beet and goat cheese salad often served in restaurants. It is a salad I love, and one that translates so well to a cocktail hors d'oeuvre. I use small glass tea light containers to make the bite-size gelatins, which can truly be eaten in one bite.

Vegetable oil for greasing the molds

2 cups (473 ml) beet juice (see Notes)

2 teaspoons agar agar powder

1¾ cups (415 ml) heavy cream

8 ounces (227 g) fresh goat cheese

1 teaspoon fine sea salt

¼ cup (15 g) fresh chives

22 water crackers or other small toasts or crackers

¼ cup (32 g) chopped candied walnuts (optional; see Notes)

Prep the Molds

Lightly coat the interior of twenty-two bite-size molds with vegetable oil. Set aside.

Make the Beet Bites

1 Place 1 cup (237 ml) of the beet juice in a small saucepan. Sprinkle the agar agar powder over the top and set aside to bloom for 10 minutes.

2 Transfer to low heat and add the cream, goat cheese, and salt along with the remaining 1 cup (237 ml) of beet juice. Cook, stirring constantly, until the gelatin has dissolved completely and the cheese has melted into the liquid, about 5 minutes.

(continued)

3 Remove from the heat and pour through a fine-mesh sieve into a bowl. Stir in the chives. Carefully spoon the mixture into the prepared molds, smoothing the tops as you go. Refrigerate until completely set, about 2 hours.

Unmold Them

1 Working with one at a time, quickly place each mold into a small bowl of hot water to come just up to but not over the edge. Hold until just beginning to loosen, about 5 seconds. Watch carefully as you do not want the gelatin to begin melting. Remove the mold from the hot water and wipe the exterior dry.

2 Place a water cracker over the mold and invert the mold onto it. The bite should pop right out.

3 Sprinkle the top of each bite with chopped candied walnuts, if using, and serve immediately.

Notes Bottled beet juice is available at most supermarkets. Fresh beet juice is also found at juice bars and many smoothie shops.

Candied walnuts are available from many supermarkets, confectionery shops, or online. See Sources, page 163.

Sweet and Yammy

MAKES SIX 6-OUNCE (177 ML) RAMEKINS

I know, I know—yams and sweet potatoes are not the same thing. But I ask you to indulge me since I call this recipe "yammy" even though I use sweet potatoes. It just sounds better. This is a perfect Thanksgiving side dish as it can be made ahead and doesn't have to be served hot. The creamy, slightly sugary sweet potato mixture can be made and placed into the ramekins a couple of days prior to the holiday, then brought to room temperature before topping and serving. This really is a fancy version of the traditional holiday sweet potato casserole.

"YAM" GELATIN

3 large (about 1 pound/454 g each) sweet potatoes, peeled and cut into large pieces (see Notes)

Salt

½ cup (118 ml) milk

1 packet (7 g) unflavored gelatin powder, such as Knox brand

1 cup (237 ml) heavy cream

½ cup (107 g) dark brown sugar

1 tablespoon unsalted butter

½ teaspoon grated nutmeg

¼ teaspoon pure vanilla extract

MARSHMALLOW TOPPING

1 cup (200 g) sugar

½ cup (118 ml) light corn syrup

Pinch of salt

1 cup (237 ml) water

2 packets (7 g each) unflavored gelatin powder, such as Knox brand

½ tablespoon pure vanilla extract

Salted pecan pieces (optional)

Make the "Yam" Gelatin

1 Place the sweet potatoes in a large saucepan. Add cold water to cover. Place over high heat, season with salt, and bring to a boil. Lower the heat and cook at a gentle simmer until very tender, about 20 minutes. Remove from the heat and drain well.

2 Spoon the sweet potatoes into the bowl of a food processor fitted with the metal blade. Process on high until very smooth and lump-free. Scrape the potatoes into a large bowl and set aside.

3 Place the milk in a medium saucepan. Sprinkle the gelatin over the top and set aside to bloom for 10 minutes.

4 Place the milk mixture over medium heat and cook, stirring, until the gelatin has dissolved completely, about 4 minutes. Add the cream, brown sugar, butter, nutmeg, vanilla, and a pinch of salt. Continue to cook, stirring occasionally, until the mixture is well blended, about 4 minutes. Add the hot mixture to the sweet potatoes, stirring to blend completely.

5 Spoon an equal portion of the sweet potato gelatin into each of six shallow ramekins, gently smoothing the top with a spatula. Place in the refrigerator until completely set, about 2 hours.

Make the Marshmallow Topping

1 Combine the sugar, corn syrup, and salt in a medium saucepan. Add ½ cup (118 ml) of the water and place over medium heat. Cook, stirring constantly, until the sugar has dissolved completely, about 5 minutes. Raise the heat to high and cook, stirring occasionally, until the mixture reaches 240°F (115°C) on a candy thermometer. Immediately remove from the heat.

2 While the syrup is cooking, place the remaining ½ cup (118 ml) of water in the bowl of a standing electric mixer. Sprinkle the gelatin over the top and let bloom for 10 minutes.

3 Attach the whisk attachment to the mixer. With the motor running on low, slowly add the hot sugar syrup to the gelatin. When all the syrup has been added, raise the speed to high and whip until very thick and it holds stiff peaks, about 15 minutes. Add the vanilla and whip to incorporate. You can make the topping right before serving or up to 2 hours before (storing covered at room temperature).

(continued)

Finish and Serve

1 Remove the "yam" gelatins from the refrigerator about an hour before serving to allow them to come to room temperature. Carefully spoon the marshmallow over the gelatins, covering the entire top with a nice thick layer; you may have some leftover (see Notes). Using a spoon, pull the marshmallow topping into peaks. If using a kitchen torch, use it to toast the marshmallow garnish (do this just before serving).

2 Sprinkle a few pecan pieces on top, if using, and serve.

Notes You could, of course, use yams if they are your preference. However, their flesh is much starchier and drier than the luscious, soft sweet potato.

You'll have leftover Marshmallow Topping, to which you can add a bit of crispy cereal and set on the counter for a few hours to turn into a crunchy cereal treat. Alternatively, spoon it over some hot coffee or cocoa to drink while you finish cooking.

Peak Lemony Asparagus

MAKES TWO 12-OUNCE (355 ML) SOUFFLÉ DISHES

When asparagus is in season this is a perfect springtime luncheon dish, light yet satisfying. Soufflé dishes, with their high walls, work well here. The varying heights of the asparagus make an unusual but very eye-catching presentation. Try to use asparagus stalks that are of a medium size; too small and they won't stand properly, too large and there won't be enough variation in heights.

Vegetable oil for greasing the soufflé dishes

3 pounds (1.4 kg) asparagus

2 tablespoons kosher salt

1 tablespoon unsalted butter

1 teaspoon minced garlic

2 cups (473 ml) clear vegetable broth

2 teaspoons agar agar powder

Juice of 1 lemon

Salt and pepper

Prep the Molds

Lightly coat the interior of two 12-ounce (355 ml) soufflé dishes with vegetable oil. Set aside.

Make the Asparagus

1 Cut the asparagus stalks to 3-inch (7.62 cm) lengths. Reserve the trimmings.

2 Prepare an ice-water bath in a large bowl (see box, page 127). Set aside.

3 Add the kosher salt to a large pot of water over high heat. Bring to a boil. Add the 3-inch (7.62) asparagus pieces and blanch until just barely cooked, 2 to 4 minutes. Drain the asparagus and immediately plunge the stalks into the ice-water bath. Chill for a minute or two to stop the cooking. Drain well and pat dry.

(continued)

Make the Jellied Broth

1 Place the butter in a medium saucepan over medium heat. Add the garlic and cook, stirring constantly, until it begins to color. Add the broth along with the asparagus trimmings. Bring to a boil, cover, and lower the heat. Simmer until the asparagus trimmings are very soft and the broth is well flavored, about 30 minutes.

2 Remove from the heat and, using an immersion blender, blend until completely smooth. (Alternately, place the broth and trimmings in a regular blender and puree until very smooth.) You should have 1½ cups (355 ml) of liquid. If necessary, add additional vegetable broth to make 1½ cups (355 ml).

3 Sprinkle the agar agar powder over the hot broth and let bloom for 10 minutes.

4 Return the broth to medium heat and bring to a simmer. Add the lemon juice and season with salt and pepper. Remove from the heat and set aside.

Build the Layers

1 Pour an equal portion of the jellied broth into each soufflé dish until half of each dish is filled.

2 Working with one dish at a time, arrange the asparagus stalks, mixing tips and stalks or separating them as pictured, to fill each dish.

3 Fill any space left in the dishes with the remaining jellied broth, taking care that it does not spill over the edge. The jellied broth will hold the asparagus firmly when unmolded. Refrigerate until completely set, about 3 hours or no more than 8 hours.

Unmold Them

1 Working with one at a time, place the soufflé dish into a bowl of hot water until just beginning to loosen, about 5 seconds. Watch carefully as you do not want the agar agar to begin melting.

2 Remove the mold from the water and wipe the exterior dry. Carefully turn the dish upside down and flip the entire mold out onto your hand. Immediately flip it right side up onto a small plate.

3 Serve immediately.

Creamy Split Pea Bites

MAKES 24 BITES

I know this seems an unusual way to sip soup, but it works beautifully. These cocktail bites are easy to eat, taste yummy, and are good for you, too. The pancetta or bacon garnish adds just the right hint of saltiness, so although it is not necessary, it does add a lovely finish. I use small glass tea-light containers as molds for the gelatins for ultimate pop-ability.

1 cup (225 g) dried split peas, rinsed

3 cups (710 ml) low-sodium chicken broth or water, plus more as needed

1 cup (52 g) diced onion

1 cup (120 g) chopped carrot

1 teaspoon grated fresh ginger

1 teaspoon minced garlic

¼ teaspoon ground cumin

Salt and pepper

2 teaspoons agar agar powder

Vegetable oil for greasing the molds

24 crackers or small toasts

24 thin pieces crisp pancetta or bacon for topping (optional)

Make the Split Pea Soup

1 Place the peas in a medium saucepan. Add the chicken broth and stir to blend. Add the onion, carrot, ginger, garlic, and cumin and place over high heat. Bring to a boil, then immediately lower the heat to a gentle simmer. Season with salt and pepper and cook, stirring frequently to keep the peas from sticking to the bottom of the pan, until the peas are mushy and the vegetables are very soft, about 1 hour. You may have to add more liquid if the soup thickens before the peas have softened.

2 Remove the pea soup from the heat and sprinkle the agar agar over the top. Set aside to bloom for 10 minutes.

3 Return the pea soup mixture to medium heat and cook, stirring, until the agar agar is fully incorporated, about 5 minutes.

Prep the Molds and Chill

1 While the soup mixture is heating, lightly coat the interior of twenty-four bite-size molds with vegetable oil. Place the greased molds on a rimmed baking sheet.

2 Pour the hot soup into a blender jar and, using a folded kitchen towel to hold the lid down (this will keep the heat and steam from pushing the lid up), process until very smooth. Spoon the hot soup into each of the prepared molds, gently smoothing the top. Refrigerate until set, about 3 hours.

Unmold and Top the Bites

1 Working with one at a time, quickly place the bottom of each mold into a small bowl of hot water until just beginning to loosen, about 5 seconds. Watch carefully as you do not want the mixture to begin melting. Remove the mold from the water and wipe the exterior dry.

2 Place a cracker over the mold and invert the mold onto it. The bite should pop right out. If using, nestle the piece of crisp pancetta or bacon into the top of each bite and serve immediately.

Lox and Lox of Everything

MAKES 24 BITES

I've turned the standard bagel and lox combination into a delicious, jelled party hors d'oeuvre. I make it in small domes and serve each atop a cucumber slice, but it would be equally delicious as a spread on bagels or pita chips. For the latter, you could set the mix in a larger mold (about 4 cups/1 L) and then unmold it onto a platter surrounded by the chips.

To make the mini domes, you will need a twenty-four-cavity semispherical silicone mold with a capacity of at least 1.25 ounces per cavity. It's available from kitchenware stores or online (see Sources, page 163).

Vegetable oil for greasing the molds

¼ cup (59 ml) water

1¼ teaspoons (4 g) unflavored gelatin powder, such as Knox brand

1 cup (237 ml) heavy cream

1 pound (454 g) cream cheese, at room temperature

2 teaspoons strained fresh lemon juice

½ teaspoon black pepper

8 ounces (227 g) smoked salmon, finely chopped

¼ cup (1.8 g) minced fresh chives

24 cucumber slices

Everything bagel seasoning for garnish

Prep the Molds

Lightly coat the interior of the cavity of each of the twenty-four semispherical dome molds with vegetable oil. Set aside.

Make the Lox Gelatin

1 Place the water in a small saucepan. Sprinkle the gelatin over the top and set aside to bloom for 10 minutes.

2 Add the heavy cream and transfer the saucepan to low heat. Cook, stirring constantly, until the gelatin has dissolved completely, about 5 minutes. Remove from the heat and pour into a medium mixing bowl.

3 Add the cream cheese, lemon juice, and pepper and, using a handheld electric mixer, beat until smooth. Add the salmon and chives and, using a rubber spatula, fold them into the cream cheese mixture. Take care that the salmon and chives are evenly distributed throughout.

4 Spoon the mixture into the prepared mold cavities and wrap the entire mold with plastic film. Return to the refrigerator and let set for 3 hours or no more than 24 hours.

Unmold Them

1 Remove the mold form from the refrigerator. Remove and discard the plastic film. Place the entire mold form in a larger rimmed pan filled with hot water to loosen for about 15 seconds, taking care that the water does not come up over the edge of the mold. Watch carefully as you do not want the gelatin to begin melting. Remove the mold from the water and wipe the exterior dry.

2 Place a serving plate over the mold form and invert the mold form onto it. The individual domes should pop right out.

3 Carefully transfer each small lox dome to a cucumber slice, flat side down. Place on a serving tray or platter. Sprinkle the top of each with everything bagel seasoning and serve immediately.

Corn and Crab Tomato Aspic

MAKES SIX 8-OUNCE (237 ML) RAMEKINS OR SOUP CUPS

Tomato aspic has a long history in America. It was an in-demand feature at early white-tablecloth restaurants, such as the famous Delmonico's in New York City. By the mid-twentieth century, it was the star of Junior League, country club, and bridge club lunches. Today, it is almost forgotten, but I am determined to bring it back! Here it is the base for a very elegant appetizer made in individual ramekins. When unmolded, the tomato aspic layer will be the bottom layer with the corn layer covering it. The crabmeat will be the very delicious garnish.

Vegetable oil for greasing the ramekins

CORN GELATIN

Freshly shaved kernels from 4 ears yellow corn (see Note)

1 tablespoon unsalted butter

Pinch of sea salt

2 packets (7 g each) unflavored gelatin powder, such as Knox brand

TOMATO ASPIC

3 cups (710 ml) tomato juice

2 packets (7 g each) unflavored gelatin powder, such as Knox brand

1½ tablespoons strained fresh lemon juice

1½ teaspoons dark brown sugar

1½ teaspoons fine sea salt

1½ teaspoons Old Bay Seasoning

½ teaspoon hot sauce

½ teaspoon finely grated lemon zest

TOPPING

8 ounces (227 g) lump crabmeat, carefully picked clean of any shell or cartilage

About 1 teaspoon fresh lemon juice

Fine sea salt

1 tablespoon chopped fresh chives

Prep the Molds

Lightly coat the interior of each of six 8-ounce (237 ml) ramekins with vegetable oil. Set aside.

(continued)

Make the Corn Gelatin

1 Place the corn in a food processor fitted with the metal blade and pulse into a chunky mix. Scrape from the processor bowl into a medium saucepan. Add the butter and salt and place over medium-high heat. Bring to a bare simmer and cook just until the butter has melted, about 1 minute. Remove from the heat and sprinkle the gelatin over the top. Set aside for 10 minutes to allow the gelatin to bloom. Then, return to low heat and cook, stirring constantly, until the gelatin has dissolved, about 5 minutes.

2 Divide the corn mixture among each of the six prepared ramekins, to come about one-third of the way up. Refrigerate until completely set, about 2 hours.

Make the Tomato Aspic

1 Place ½ cup (118 ml) of the tomato juice in a medium mixing bowl. Sprinkle the gelatin over the top and set aside to bloom for 10 minutes.

2 Combine the remaining tomato juice with the lemon juice, brown sugar, salt, Old Bay Seasoning, hot sauce, and lemon zest in a medium saucepan over low heat. Cook, stirring frequently, until well blended and hot, about 5 minutes. Remove from the heat, add the gelatin mixture, and stir until the gelatin has dissolved completely. Return the mixture to the medium mixing bowl and refrigerate until well chilled and thickened but not completely set, about 1 hour.

Build the Layers and Prep the Topping

1 Remove the ramekins from the refrigerator and spoon an equal portion of the chilled tomato aspic mixture into each, filling to the top to completely cover the corn layer. Tightly cover each ramekin with plastic film and return to the refrigerator. Chill until completely set, about 2 hours or no more than 8 hours.

2 When almost time to serve, place the crabmeat in a small dish, taking care that there are no remaining pieces of shell or cartilage. Add the lemon juice and salt, tossing to season well. Taste and, if necessary, add additional lemon and/or salt.

Unmold Them

1 Remove and discard the plastic film. Working with one at a time, quickly place the ramekin into a small bowl of hot water to come up to but not over the edge. Hold until just beginning to loosen, about 5 seconds. Watch carefully as you do not want the gelatin to begin melting. Remove the ramekin from the water and wipe the exterior dry. Place a small plate over the ramekin and invert the ramekin onto it. The aspic should pop right out. Transfer it to the refrigerator while you unmold the remaining ramekins.

2 When all the aspics have been unmolded and plated, remove from the refrigerator, and place an equal portion of the seasoned crabmeat atop each one. Garnish with a sprinkle of chives and serve immediately.

Note To cut the kernels off the corn, first remove the husks and all silk from each ear. Working with one ear at a time, hold the ear straight in the center of a large shallow bowl. Using a sharp chef's knife, in a downward motion slice off the kernels. You want to catch all kernels and any corn milk. You should have 2 cups (175 g) of corn.

Variation Simple Tomato Aspic: The slightly acidic tomato marries perfectly with sweet corn and luscious crabmeat, but it is so refreshing by itself, you could easily double that portion of the recipe to serve six people on its own. The 8-ounce ramekins (or soup cups, if you prefer) will be large enough to accommodate a double portion. Serve it garnished with chopped herbs, a lemon slice, or a poached shrimp.

Caramelized Carrot Panna Cotta

MAKES SIX 6-OUNCE (177 ML) CRÈME BRÛLÉE RAMEKINS OR TWELVE 3-OUNCE (88 ML) MOLDS

This is an unusual appetizer—slightly sweet, but still intriguingly savory. The sweetness of the roasted, caramelized carrots balances the zing of the herbs and spices. I usually make this in small ramekins or molds, but you could also use four slightly larger ramekins and center the finished panna cotta on a plate of beautiful Bibb lettuce leaves for a luncheon main course.

Unflavored vegetable oil for greasing the ramekins

ROASTED CARROTS

2 tablespoons unsalted butter, melted

2 tablespoons honey

4 large (about 1 pound/454 g) carrots, peeled, trimmed, and cut into chunks

1 tablespoon olive oil

Sea salt

PANNA COTTA

1¾ cups (415 ml) water

2 sprigs flat-leaf parsley

1 stalk celery, trimmed and cut into chunks

1 sprig (2 inches/5 cm) fresh rosemary

1 bay leaf

½ teaspoon peppercorns

¼ teaspoon allspice berries

1 tablespoon agar agar flakes or 1 teaspoon agar agar powder

1 teaspoon salt or to taste

¼ cup (59 ml) heavy cream

2 tablespoons soft goat cheese

Hot sauce to taste

Dehydrated carrot chips for garnish (optional; see Note)

Prep the Molds

1 Place an oven rack in the center of the oven and preheat the oven to 400°F (204°C). Line a rimmed baking sheet with a silicone liner or nonstick aluminum foil. Set aside.

2 Lightly coat the interior of six 6-ounce (177 ml) crème brûlée ramekins or twelve 3-ounce (88 ml) molds with vegetable oil. Set aside.

(continued)

Make the Roasted Carrots

1 Combine the melted butter and honey in a small bowl, whisking to blend completely. Place all but 6 chunks of the carrots onto the prepared baking sheet and drizzle with the olive oil, tossing to coat. Drizzle with the honey butter, again tossing to coat, and season with sea salt.

2 Roast, turning occasionally, until lightly colored and very tender, but not falling apart, about 20 minutes. Remove from the oven and set aside to cool.

Make the Panna Cotta

1 Place the water in a medium saucepan. Add the remaining 6 carrot chunks along with the parsley, celery, rosemary, bay leaf, peppercorns, and allspice. Stir in the agar agar along with the salt and place over high heat. Bring to a simmer, stirring frequently to keep the agar agar from sticking to the bottom of the pan. Immediately lower the heat and cook at a bare simmer, continuing to stir frequently so that the agar agar does not settle onto the bottom of the pan, until the broth is very aromatic, about 15 minutes. Remove from the heat and let cool for 10 minutes.

2 Transfer the cooled roasted carrots to a high-speed blender, such as a Vitamix. Pour the agar agar broth through a fine-mesh sieve into the blender. Add the cream, goat cheese, and hot sauce and process until very smooth, pausing to scrape down the sides of the blender jar from time to time. Taste and, if necessary, season with additional salt and hot sauce.

3 Pour an equal portion of the carrot puree into each of the prepared ramekins. When filled, lift each ramekin and gently plop it down a couple of times to eliminate any bubbles and allow the puree to settle evenly. Set aside at room temperature until completely set, about 1 hour. If you want to serve the panna cotta warm, place it in a preheated 350°F (177°C) oven for about 5 minutes or until just warmed through.

Unmold Them

1 Working with one at a time, quickly place the ramekin into a small bowl of hot water until just beginning to loosen, about 5 seconds. Watch carefully as you do not want the panna cotta to begin melting. Remove the ramekin from the water and wipe the exterior dry.

2 Place a luncheon plate over the ramekin and invert the ramekin onto it. The panna cotta should pop right out.

3 Repeat with the remaining panna cottas. Nestle a carrot chip, if using, into the center of each and serve immediately.

Note Dehydrated carrot chips are available at health food stores, many supermarkets, specialty food shops, and online.

Potato-Salmon Terrine

MAKES ONE 12-INCH (30 CM) TERRINE

This fancy terrine makes a terrific centerpiece for a summer luncheon. It is light yet substantial and, oh, so elegant. It can be served with a small salad, a light vinaigrette, or simply as is, fresh and delicious. Don't be put off by the number of steps—each one is easy to accomplish, and the final dish is worth the effort. Lining the terrine with plastic film rather than greasing it ensures that you can easily lift the loaf out of the pan. The terrine can be made a day or so in advance, which I love as it results in a relaxed cook on the day of service.

POTATOES AND LEEKS

15 medium new potatoes, peeled

6 cups (1.4 L) low-sodium, fat-free chicken broth

4 cloves garlic

4 sprigs fresh thyme

2 bay leaves

Salt and black pepper

3 medium leeks, well washed and trimmed, root ends removed

ASPIC

2 packets (7 g each) unflavored gelatin powder, such as Knox brand

1 tablespoon minced fresh dill

SALMON

2½ pounds (1 kg) skinless, boneless salmon (or other firm fish) fillet

Salt and pepper

2 tablespoons peanut oil

Prep the Pan

Line a 12 × 4 × 4-inch (30 × 10 × 10 cm) loaf pan or terrine with plastic film, allowing a 2- to 3-inch (5 to 7.62 cm) overhang all around and taking care that the film lies flat on all sides. Set aside.

(continued)

Make the Potatoes and Leeks

1 Place the potatoes in a large saucepan. Add 4 cups (1 L) of the broth, 2 cloves of the garlic, 2 sprigs of the thyme, and 1 of the bay leaves. Season with salt and pepper and place over high heat. Bring to a boil and immediately lower the heat to a gentle simmer. Cook until the potatoes are tender when pierced with the point of a small, sharp knife, about 20 minutes.

2 Remove from the heat and drain through a fine-mesh sieve into a clean bowl, separately reserving the potatoes and cooking liquid. Discard the garlic, thyme, and bay leaf. Cut the potatoes into very thin (about ⅛-inch/3 mm-thick) slices and lay out on a flat platter. Cover with plastic film and set aside.

3 Using a sharp knife, cut the leeks in half lengthwise. Peel off each layer and rinse well under cold running water; pat dry. Place the leeks in a large saucepan. Add the remaining 2 cups (473 ml) of broth along with the remaining garlic, thyme, and bay leaf. Season with salt and place over medium heat. Cook until just tender and very pliable, about 4 minutes.

4 Remove from the heat and drain through a fine-mesh sieve, separately reserving the leeks and the cooking liquid. Discard the garlic, thyme, and bay leaf.

Make the Aspic

1 Combine the reserved potato cooking liquid with the leek cooking liquid in a medium saucepan. Place over medium heat and cook at a gentle simmer until reduced to 4 cups (1 L), about 15 minutes. Taste and, if necessary, season with salt and pepper. Keep warm.

2 Place ½ cup (118 ml) of the warm cooking liquid in a medium saucepan. Add the gelatin and set aside to bloom for 5 minutes. Transfer to low heat and cook, stirring frequently, until the gelatin has completely dissolved, about 3 minutes. Add the remaining cooking liquid along with the dill, stirring to blend. Remove from the heat and keep warm.

Make the Salmon

1 Cut the salmon into pieces about ½ inch (1.27 cm) thick and 2 inches (5 cm) wide. You should have enough to make 3 layers that will cover the length and width of the terrine. Season with salt and pepper.

2 Place the peanut oil in a medium, nonstick frying pan over medium-high heat. When the oil is very hot, but not smoking, add the salmon and sear for 1 minute. Turn and sear the remaining side for another minute. The salmon should remain almost raw in the center.

3 Remove from the pan and set on a double layer of paper towel to drain. Then immediately place on a plate and transfer to the refrigerator to stop the cooking.

Assemble the Terrine

1 Spoon enough of the aspic into the prepared terrine to cover the bottom with a thin layer. Carefully place the sliced potatoes into a large shallow bowl. Add ½ cup (118 ml) of the aspic to just moisten the potatoes. Set aside.

2 Place 1 cup (237 ml) of the remaining aspic in a shallow bowl. Working with one piece at a time, dip the leeks into the aspic and carefully line the bottom and the sides of the terrine with a single layer, allowing the leeks on the sides to overhang by 2 inches (5 cm); reserve the remaining leeks. Add a single layer of the moistened potatoes atop the leeks on the bottom.

3 Cut a salmon piece, lengthwise, into 3 equal pieces. Layer the salmon pieces over the potatoes. Add about ¼ cup (59 ml) of the aspic and, using your fingertips, press down on the salmon and potatoes to make a compressed, neat layer. Continue making layers of potatoes, salmon, and aspic and pressing down as you go, ending with a final layer of potatoes and aspic. Press down firmly to make sure the aspic covers the potatoes.

4 Layer the reserved leek pieces over the final potato layer. Then, bring the leek overhang up and over the top to enclose the terrine. Add any remaining aspic and press down to eliminate any air pockets and to ensure that the aspic covers the potatoes and salmon and seeps into any empty spaces. Fold the plastic film up and over the top of the terrine to enclose tightly. Refrigerate until completely set, at least 8 hours or up to 24 hours.

Unmold It

1 When ready to serve, remove the terrine from the refrigerator. Lift up the plastic film and, holding firmly, lift the entire terrine out of the container. Unwrap and place on a cutting board.

2 Using a serrated knife, slowly and carefully cut the terrine into slices about ½ inch (1.27 cm) thick. Serve immediately.

Fluke Crudo Tostadas
with Tomato Gelée and Avocado Mousse

MAKES 6 TOSTADAS

This is an amazing way to begin a festive meal. These fluke tostadas are light yet satisfying with just a hint of chile heat in the gelée. The marvelous flavors of the almost sweet fish, the spicy tomato, and the creamy avocado with the crisp tostada come together to create an almost intoxicating blend. They could easily serve as a light luncheon treat also, but guests just might want to have more than one.

TOMATO GELÉE

1 cup (237 ml) tomato juice

1 clove garlic, smashed

1 Calabrian chile (see Notes)

2 sheets gelatin, torn into pieces

½ cup (118 ml) water

2½ tablespoons (37 ml) sherry vinegar

Pinch of sea salt

AVOCADO MOUSSE AND FLUKE

1 ripe avocado

Juice and zest of 1 lime

Sea salt

1 pound (454 g) very fresh fluke fillet or any other flaky white fish, thinly sliced on the bias

Juice of 1 lemon

1½ tablespoons extra-virgin olive oil

TO FINISH

6 corn tostadas (see Notes)

Zest and juice of 1 lemon

Sea salt

6 leaves basil, torn into small pieces

Make the Tomato Gelée

1 Combine the tomato juice, garlic, and chile in a small bowl. Cover with plastic film and place in the refrigerator to infuse for 8 hours.

2 When ready to make the gelée, place the gelatin pieces in a small bowl. Add the water and set aside to bloom for 10 minutes.

3 Remove the tomato juice mixture from the refrigerator and strain through a fine-mesh sieve into a small saucepan. Add the vinegar and salt. Place over medium heat and bring to a boil.

4 Lift the gelatin pieces from the water, carefully squeeze the excess water from them, and add them to the boiling juice. Return to a boil, stirring to dissolve the gelatin. Remove from the heat and strain through a fine-mesh sieve onto a plate or small rimmed baking sheet. Let the gelée come to room temperature, then refrigerate until just set but not firm, about 1 hour.

Make the Avocado Mousse and Fluke

1 Place the avocado and the lime juice and zest in the bowl of a small food processor fitted with the metal blade. Season with sea salt. Pulse into a smooth puree (take care not to overprocess as the mousse will become too loose). Scrape the mixture into a small bowl, cover tightly with plastic film, and place in the refrigerator.

2 Combine the thinly sliced fluke with the lemon juice and olive oil in a large shallow bowl. Season lightly with salt.

Finish the Dish

1 Place the corn tostadas on a clean work surface. Working with one at a time, carefully lay the fish slices, slightly overlapping, over the top of each tostada. Sprinkle with a bit of lemon zest and lemon juice. Season lightly with salt.

2 Remove the tomato gelée and avocado mousse from the refrigerator. Dollop small amounts of each randomly over the fish.

3 Garnish with a few pieces of basil leaf, place on a small plate, and serve immediately.

Notes Calabrian chiles are available, canned, from Italian markets, specialty food stores, some supermarkets, and online. They are medium hot with a slightly sweet, smoky flavor.

Tostadas are packaged crisp fried tortillas that are available from Latin markets, specialty food stores, some supermarkets, and online. They are served flat with various toppings. If you can't find tostadas, you can fry corn tortillas in hot oil just until crisp.

Chapter 4

Time for Drinks

Jiggly Bellini

MAKES 8 TO 10 INDIVIDUAL GLASSES OR ONE 2-QUART (2 L) MOLD

This is my very tasty take on that brunchtime favorite, a bellini. It is a luscious mix of champagne and peaches made famous at Harry's Bar in Venice, Italy. Presenting the bellinis in champagne or wine glasses, complete with light-catching gold leaf, will ensure every person at your table gets their very own disco ball–like treat. Alternatively, you could prepare the recipe in a 2-quart (2 L) mold and serve it as the opening act for a lavish brunch or weekend lunch (see Note). Whatever you decide to do, the result will WOW! When unmolding the large mold, the champagne layer will be the top layer and the nectar layer will be the base.

Vegetable oil for greasing the mold

PEACH NECTAR GELATIN

7 sheets gelatin, broken into pieces

¼ cup (59 ml) champagne or prosecco

2¾ cups (651 ml) pure peach nectar, chilled

2 teaspoons edible gold glitter

CHAMPAGNE GELATIN

5 sheets gelatin, broken into pieces, use platinum grade for ultimate clarity

2 cups (473 ml) champagne or prosecco

3 tablespoons (36 g) superfine sugar

Juice of ½ lemon, well strained of any pulp

25 sheets edible gold leaf

One 15-ounce (425 g) can sliced peaches in juice, well drained and patted dry

Make the Peach Nectar Gelatin

1 Place the gelatin pieces in a small saucepan. Add the champagne and set aside for 10 minutes to bloom. Place the saucepan over low heat and cook, stirring constantly, until the gelatin has completely dissolved, about 5 minutes. Remove from the heat and cool to room temperature. When cool, stir in the peach nectar and glitter.

(continued)

2 Spoon the peach nectar gelatin into each glass until it is evenly distributed among them. Carefully place them in the refrigerator until set, 1 to 2 hours.

Make the Champagne Gelatin

1 Place the gelatin pieces into a heatproof bowl. Add just enough champagne to cover and set aside to bloom for 10 minutes. Place the remainder of the champagne into a medium bowl and set aside.

2 Set up a double boiler and ice-water bath (see box, page 127); set the ice-water bath aside.

3 Place the heatproof bowl of gelatin onto the double boiler and heat, stirring occasionally, until the gelatin has completely dissolved, about 4 minutes. Add the sugar and continue to heat, stirring gently and constantly, until the sugar has dissolved, about another 3 minutes. Stir in the lemon juice and remove the bowl from the heat.

4 Place a fine-mesh sieve over the bowl of reserved champagne and pour the hot gelatin mixture through it. Stir to blend completely, then transfer the bowl to the ice-water bath.

5 Add the gold leaf, stirring constantly until the gelatin begins to set. (You want the gold leaf to remain suspended throughout.)

Build the Layers

1 Remove the glasses from the refrigerator and carefully scoop the champagne gelatin into each glass.

2 Place the glasses back in the refrigerator until the second layer is semi-firm and set just enough to hold the peach slices, about 30 minutes.

3 Remove the glasses from the refrigerator once more, and carefully insert one peach slice into the top layer of each glass. You want the peach slices to stay suspended in the gelatin. Refrigerate until set, about 2 hours.

4 Serve in the glasses.

Note If you want to make a large mold rather than individual glasses, you'll want to remember to lightly grease your mold with vegetable oil. Since the large mold is to be unmolded, you'll also want to reverse the order of layers, so the champagne layer should go into the mold first, followed by the peach nectar layer. When ready to unmold, place the mold in a bowl of hot water for 15 to 30 seconds to loosen it up a bit. Wipe the mold dry, place a serving plate over the mold, and quickly invert it. Slice to serve.

Double Boilers and Ice-Water Baths

A **double boiler** is useful when you want to gently heat your ingredients. To make one, simply find a saucepan that's just large enough to suspend the heatproof bowl a couple of inches above the bottom of the pan. Add water to the pan to reach a depth of 1 to 2 inches (2.5 to 5 cm)—you want it to heat the bowlful of ingredients without touching the bowl directly. Bring the water to a boil over medium heat.

An **ice-water bath** will cool down your ingredients quickly and is constructed in a similar fashion. Place a good amount of ice and some water in a bowl large enough to comfortably hold the heatproof bowl (without allowing any water to overflow into the bowl). Set aside.

PB & Jiggle Shot

MAKES 8 SHOTS

This is an adult take on the classic peanut butter and jelly combination that so many of us loved as kids. The peanut butter flavor flows from the unusual whiskey, which makes it very grown-up, indeed. To serve the shots, you will need either eight real shot glasses or disposable ones. Since I am always experimenting with gelatin drinks, I like to use biodegradable disposable shot glasses (available online).

2 cups (473 ml) organic grape juice

1 packet (7 g) unflavored gelatin powder, such as Knox brand

¼ cup (59 ml) Skrewball Peanut Butter Whiskey

¼ teaspoon edible iridescent glitter

1 Place 1 cup (237 ml) of the grape juice in a small saucepan. Sprinkle the gelatin over the top and set aside to bloom for 10 minutes.

2 Place the saucepan over low heat and stir in the whiskey along with the remaining 1 cup (237 ml) of grape juice. Cook, stirring constantly, until the gelatin has dissolved completely, about 4 minutes. Remove from the heat and pour through a fine-mesh sieve into a large liquid measuring cup. Refrigerate until the gelatin begins to set, about 30 minutes.

3 Remove the gelatin from the refrigerator and add the glitter, stirring to distribute it throughout. Pour an equal portion of the gelatin into each of eight 2-ounce (59 ml) shot glasses and return to the refrigerator until completely set, about 30 minutes or for no more than 12 hours.

4 Serve in the shot glasses.

Mom's Pometini

MAKES SIX 6-OUNCE (177 ML) MARTINI GLASSES

Yes, here's another one for Mom! What can I say except she's my favorite girl. She isn't much of a drinker until it comes time for a pomegranate martini. She can down one faster than the bartender can make it! This recipe makes six sweet and boozy after-dinner "drinks" or can also be made into bite-size portions for an elevated take on a JELL-O shot.

3 cups (710 ml) pomegranate juice

6 sheets gelatin, torn into small pieces

3 ounces (88 ml) citrus-infused vodka

2 ounces (59 ml) Cointreau liqueur

¼ cup (50 g) sugar

2 tablespoons fresh lemon juice, strained

½ cup (40 g) pomegranate arils for garnish (optional)

1 tablespoon edible silver glitter for garnish (optional)

1 Place 1 cup (237 ml) of the pomegranate juice in a medium saucepan. Add the gelatin and set aside to bloom for 10 minutes.

2 Add the remaining 2 cups (473 ml) of pomegranate juice and place over low heat. Cook, stirring constantly, until the gelatin has dissolved completely, about 5 minutes. Remove from the heat and add the vodka, Cointreau, sugar, and lemon juice, stirring constantly until the sugar has dissolved completely, about 5 minutes. Set aside to come to room temperature.

3 Ladle the mixture into each of six martini glasses, dividing it evenly. Refrigerate until completely set, about 3 hours.

4 When ready to serve, place the pomegranate arils, if using, in a small resealable plastic bag. Add the glitter, seal, and shake vigorously to coat the arils. Remove the martinis from the refrigerator and sprinkle an equal portion of the glittery arils over the top of each one. Serve immediately.

Brown Derby Shots

MAKES ABOUT 10 SHOTS

Since a Brown Derby—a blend of bourbon, grapefruit juice, and honey—is one of my most favorite cocktails, I had to translate it to a gelatin shot. I love the way the honey removes the bitterness from the grapefruit but allows its sweetness to remain. The mellowness of the gelatin brings it all to perfection.

1¾ cups (415 ml) organic pink grapefruit juice

1 packet (7 g) unflavored gelatin powder, such as Knox brand

½ cup (118 ml) bourbon

½ cup (170 g) honey

½ teaspoon edible pink glitter

1 Place the grapefruit juice in a small saucepan. Sprinkle the gelatin over the top and set aside to bloom for 10 minutes.

2 Place the grapefruit juice mixture in the saucepan over low heat and add the bourbon and honey. Cook, stirring constantly, until the gelatin has dissolved completely, about 4 minutes. Pour the mixture through a fine-mesh sieve into a medium bowl. Transfer the bowl to the freezer and, stirring occasionally, let chill until beginning to thicken, about 45 minutes.

3 Remove the bowl from the freezer and gently stir in the glitter. You want it to stay suspended in the gelatin so do not overmix. Spoon the mixture into shot glasses, filling about three-quarters full. Refrigerate until set, about 1 hour.

4 Serve immediately.

Summer Fruit Rosé

MAKES ONE 1-QUART (1 L) MOLD

To me, nothing says summer more than a chilled glass of rosé wine and a bite of luscious summer fruit. My summer highlights always take place on the beach spending time with friends and sipping our favorite French rosé. This summer recipe is the perfect addition to a backyard barbecue or a casual lunch by the pool.

Vegetable oil for greasing the mold

7 sheets gelatin, broken into small pieces

½ cup (118 ml) white grape juice

One 25.4 ounce (750 ml) bottle fine-quality rosé wine

⅓ cup (79 ml) strained fresh lemon juice

3 tablespoons (45 ml) Grand Marnier

¼ cup (50 g) sugar

½ cup (62 g) fresh raspberries

8 large fresh strawberries, hulled and quartered

2 red plums, pitted and cut lengthwise into ¼-inch- (0.64 cm) thick slices

2 peaches, peeled, pitted, and cut into ¼-inch- (0.64 cm) thick slices

½ teaspoon edible pink glitter

Prep the Mold

Lightly coat the interior of a 1-quart (1 L) mold with vegetable oil. Set aside.

Make the Rosé Gelatin

1 Place the gelatin pieces in a medium saucepan. Add the grape juice and set aside to bloom for 10 minutes.

2 Add the wine to the gelatin and place over low heat. Cook, stirring constantly, until the gelatin has dissolved completely, about 4 minutes. Add the lemon juice, Grand Marnier, and sugar and continue to cook, stirring, until the sugar has dissolved completely, about 3 minutes.

(continued)

3 Remove from the heat and pour through a fine-mesh sieve into a medium bowl. Transfer the bowl to the freezer and, stirring occasionally, let chill until beginning to thicken, about 45 minutes.

4 Remove the bowl from the freezer and gently stir in the fruit and glitter. You want them to stay suspended in the gelatin so do not overmix. Spoon the thick mixture into the prepared mold. Refrigerate until completely set, about 3 hours or up to 24 hours.

Unmold It

1 Remove the mold from the refrigerator. Place the mold in a bowl of hot water for 15 to 30 seconds to loosen. Watch carefully as you do not want the gelatin to begin melting. Remove the mold from the water and wipe the exterior dry. Place a serving plate over the mold and quickly invert the mold onto it. The gelatin should pop right out.

2 Serve immediately.

Lime in the Coconut

MAKES 2 CUPS (473 ML) OR 16 SHOTS

This shot is based on a classic Brazilian limeade (limonada Suíça) that uses the entire lime. When I attempted to re-create it myself at home, I quickly learned that it is very, very important that you not overprocess or the drink will be overpoweringly bitter. When done right, it is one of the most refreshing drinks in the world.

3 organic limes, cut lengthwise into quarters

1 cup (237 ml) pressed coconut water (see Note)

½ cup (118 ml) Coco López Cream of Coconut

¼ cup (77 g) sweetened condensed milk

1 packet (7 g) unflavored gelatin powder, such as Knox brand

½ cup (118 ml) vodka

16 small lime candy wedges for garnish (optional)

Shredded or shaved coconut for garnish (optional)

1 Place the cut limes, pressed coconut water, cream of coconut, and condensed milk in a blender. Process just until broken down, but for no more than 15 seconds (do not overprocess or the drink will be bitter!). Pour the mixture through a fine-mesh sieve into a small saucepan. Sprinkle the gelatin over the top and set aside to bloom for 10 minutes.

2 Place the lime gelatin mixture in the saucepan over low heat and cook, stirring constantly, until the gelatin has dissolved, about 4 minutes. Remove from the heat and stir in the vodka. Pour the mixture through a fine-mesh sieve into a medium bowl and transfer to the freezer. Chill until the mixture has thickened somewhat, about 45 minutes.

3 Spoon an equal portion of the thickened lime gelatin into each of the sixteen shot glasses. If desired, garnish each shot glass with a lime candy wedge and a sprinkle of shredded or shaved coconut.

Note Pressed coconut water is made by pressing the meat of a coconut to create a rich, creamy liquid, whereas plain coconut water is simply the clear liquid inside the coconut.

Shot of Espresso

MAKES 1¾ CUPS (415 ML) OR ABOUT 8 SHOTS

This is a terrific drink to serve with dessert or even as dessert—the Kahlúa and added sugar make it a sweeter shot to take. They're darling in little espresso cups, if you have them. Using instant espresso eases the preparation, making this a wonderful last-minute addition to the menu.

ESPRESSO GELATIN

1 cup (237 ml) espresso coffee, at room temperature (see Note)

1 packet (7 g) unflavored gelatin powder, such as Knox brand

½ cup (118 ml) Kahlúa Coffee Liqueur

¼ cup (59 ml) vodka

¼ teaspoon edible gold glitter

CREAM GELATIN

½ cup (118 ml) heavy cream

1 teaspoon unflavored gelatin powder, such as Knox brand

2 tablespoons sugar

½ teaspoon pure vanilla extract

TO FINISH

1 teaspoon espresso powder (optional)

¼ teaspoon edible gold glitter (optional)

Make the Espresso Gelatin

1 Place the espresso in a small saucepan. Sprinkle the gelatin over the top and set aside to bloom for 10 minutes.

2 Place the saucepan over low heat and cook, stirring constantly, until the gelatin has dissolved completely, about 4 minutes. Stir in the Kahlúa and vodka and remove from the heat.

3 Pour the mixture through a fine-mesh sieve into a medium bowl. Transfer the bowl to the freezer and, stirring occasionally, let chill until beginning to thicken, about 35 minutes.

4 Remove the bowl from the freezer and gently stir in the glitter so it stays suspended in the gelatin; do not overmix. Spoon the mixture into shot glasses, filling about three-quarters full. Refrigerate until set, about 1 hour.

(continued)

Make the Cream Gelatin

1 Place the cream in a small saucepan. Sprinkle the gelatin over the top and set aside to bloom for 10 minutes.

2 Place the saucepan over low heat and cook, stirring constantly, until the gelatin has dissolved completely, about 4 minutes. Stir in the sugar and vanilla and continue to cook, stirring, until the sugar has dissolved, about 3 minutes.

3 Remove from the heat and pour the mixture through a fine-mesh sieve into a small bowl. Set aside to come to room temperature.

Finish the Shots

1 Remove the espresso shots from the refrigerator. Spoon an equal portion of the cooled cream gelatin over the top of each shot. Refrigerate until the cream layer has set, about 30 minutes.

2 Serve, garnished with a dusting of espresso powder and a sprinkle of glitter, if desired.

Note Instant espresso powder may be used to make the espresso. Follow the directions on the package.

Sweet Tiki

MAKES ONE 1-QUART (1 L) MOLD OR ABOUT 20 SHOTS

This is my take on a traditional tiki drink called the Painkiller, a mix of rum, pineapple and orange juices, cream of coconut, and a hint of nutmeg. The results are equal parts drink and dessert, so I usually make this in a large mold, although it most certainly can be served as a shot (it will make close to two dozen). When set in the larger form, I cut it into slices and ask guests to sip it off a spoon, which usually causes some mishaps and laughs.

Vegetable oil for greasing the mold

Shredded coconut (optional)

CREAMY RUM GELATIN

½ cup (118 ml) orange juice

3 packets (7 g each) unflavored gelatin powder, such as Knox brand

Juice of 2 limes

2 cups (473 ml) pineapple juice

¾ cup (177 ml) dark rum

½ cup (118 ml) Coco López Cream of Coconut

2 tablespoons maraschino cherry syrup

½ teaspoon freshly grated nutmeg

FRUIT AND GLITTER

½ cup (170 g) cubed fresh pineapple

½ cup (60 g) well-drained maraschino cherries

½ teaspoon edible iridescent white glitter

Prep the Mold

1 Lightly coat the interior of a 1-quart (1 L) mold with vegetable oil.

2 If desired, lightly coat the bottom of the mold with shredded coconut. Set aside.

Make the Creamy Rum Gelatin

1 Place the orange juice in a small saucepan. Sprinkle the gelatin over the top and set aside to bloom for 10 minutes.

(continued)

2 Add the lime juice, pineapple juice, rum, cream of coconut, maraschino syrup, and nutmeg and place over low heat. Cook, stirring constantly, until the gelatin has dissolved completely, about 4 minutes.

3 Pour the mixture through a fine-mesh sieve into a medium bowl. Transfer the bowl to the freezer and, stirring occasionally, let chill until beginning to thicken, about 45 minutes.

Add the Fruit and Glitter

1 Remove the bowl from the freezer and gently stir in the pineapple, maraschino cherries, and glitter so they are suspended throughout; do not overmix.

2 Spoon the mixture into the prepared mold. Refrigerate until completely set, about 2 hours or up to 24 hours.

Unmold It

1 Remove the mold from the refrigerator. Place the mold in a bowl of hot water for 15 to 30 seconds to loosen. Watch carefully as you do not want the gelatin to begin melting. Remove the mold from the water and wipe the exterior dry.

2 Place a serving plate over the mold and quickly invert the mold onto it. The gelatin should pop right out.

3 Cut into slices and serve immediately.

Party Cake Shots

MAKES 16 SHOTS

These shots are a great combination of flavors, rather like an adult version of the old standby ice cream pop with creamy vanilla coated in chocolate. Absolutely the best.

This recipe serves a crowd, since I've found that partygoers at my house frequently ask for seconds. These sparklingly tasty gelatin shots are sure to be a favorite at your next party, too!

VANILLA GELATIN

1½ cups (355 ml) clear cream soda, such as D&G Genuine Jamaican Cream Soda (see Sources, page 163)

1 packet (7 g) unflavored gelatin powder, such as Knox brand

¼ cup (59 ml) vanilla-flavored vodka

¼ teaspoon edible glitter, your choice of color

WHITE CHOCOLATE GELATIN

1½ cups (355 ml) heavy cream

1 packet (7 g) unflavored gelatin powder, such as Knox brand

¼ cup (50 g) sugar

¼ cup (59 ml) Godiva White Chocolate Liqueur

Make the Vanilla Gelatin

1 Place the soda in a small saucepan. Sprinkle the gelatin over the top and set aside to bloom for 10 minutes.

2 Place the saucepan over low heat and cook, stirring constantly, until the gelatin has dissolved completely, about 4 minutes. Remove from the heat and stir in the vodka. Pour the mixture through a fine-mesh sieve into a small bowl. Refrigerate until just beginning to thicken, about 30 minutes.

3 Remove from the refrigerator and add the glitter, stirring to distribute it throughout the gelatin.

4 Using about half of the vanilla mixture (set aside the rest), fill each shot glass about one-third full. Refrigerate until completely set, about 1 hour.

Make the White Chocolate Gelatin

1 Place the cream in a small saucepan. Sprinkle the gelatin over the top and set aside to bloom for 10 minutes.

2 Add the sugar and place over low heat. Cook, stirring constantly, until both the gelatin and sugar have dissolved completely, about 5 minutes. Remove from the heat and stir in the liqueur. Refrigerate the gelatin in the saucepan until it just begins to thicken, about 30 minutes.

Build the Layers

1 Remove the white chocolate gelatin and the partially filled shot glasses from the refrigerator. Spoon an equal portion of the white chocolate mixture over the set vanilla gelatin to fill each glass two-thirds full.

2 Return the shot glasses to the refrigerator and chill until completely set, about 1 hour.

3 Remove the shot glasses from the refrigerator. Using the remainder of the vanilla gelatin, spoon an equal portion into each glass. Return the glasses to the refrigerator and chill until set, about 1 hour or no more than 12 hours.

4 Serve in the shot glasses.

Mallow Limoncello

MAKES SIX 4-OUNCE (118 ML) GLASSES

Limoncello is a traditional Italian digestivo, an after-dinner drink that mellows the tummy after a hearty meal. It is strongly alcoholic and infused with lemon zest, which makes it very lemony and slightly bitter, with a deep yellow cloudiness. The drink itself is always served cold, which makes it an appropriate addition to a chilled dessert. The toasty marshmallow adds the perfect touch of sweetness to end a meal.

Vegetable oil for greasing the molds

LIMONCELLO GELATIN

2½ cups (592 ml) milk

1 packet (7 g) unflavored gelatin powder, such as Knox brand

¼ cup (50 g) sugar

½ cup (30 g) cornstarch

3 large egg yolks, lightly beaten

2 tablespoons finely grated lemon zest

Pinch of salt

½ cup (118 ml) limoncello liqueur

2 tablespoons unsalted butter, at room temperature

MARSHMALLOW TOPPING

½ cup (100 g) sugar

¼ cup (43 g) light corn syrup

Pinch of salt

1 cup (237 ml) water

1 packet (7 g) unflavored gelatin powder, such as Knox brand

1 teaspoon pure vanilla extract

Prep the Molds

Lightly coat the interior of six 4-ounce (118 ml) shallow ramekins with vegetable oil.

Make the Limoncello Gelatin

1 Place the milk in a medium saucepan. Sprinkle the gelatin over the top and set aside to bloom for 10 minutes.

2 Place the milk mixture over low heat and cook, stirring, until the gelatin has dissolved completely, about 4 minutes.

(continued)

3 Add the sugar and cornstarch and, using a whisk, beat until lump-free and smooth. Whisk in the egg yolks, zest, and salt and cook, stirring constantly, until thick enough to coat the back of a metal spoon, about 7 minutes. Remove from the heat and add the limoncello and butter, stirring to incorporate.

4 Pour the gelatin through a fine-mesh sieve into a clean bowl. Spoon an equal portion into each ramekin. Refrigerate until set, about 3 hours or up to 24 hours.

Make the Marshmallow Topping

1 Combine the sugar, corn syrup, and salt in a medium saucepan. Add ½ cup (118 ml) of the water and place over medium heat. Cook, stirring constantly, until the sugar has dissolved completely, about 5 minutes. Raise the heat to high and cook, stirring occasionally, until the mixture reaches 240°F (115°C) on a candy thermometer. Immediately remove from the heat.

2 While the syrup is cooking, place the remaining ½ cup (118 ml) of water in the bowl of a standing electric mixer with the whisk attachment. Sprinkle the gelatin over the top and let bloom for 10 minutes.

3 With the motor running on low, slowly add the hot sugar syrup to the gelatin. When all the syrup has been added, raise the speed to high and whip until the mixture is very thick and holds stiff peaks, about 15 minutes. Add the vanilla and whip to incorporate.

Build the Layers

1 Remove the limoncello gelatins from the refrigerator. Carefully spoon some of the marshmallow onto the center top of each (you will have some marshmallow leftover, see Note), pulling it into even mounds with little peaks.

2 If you have a kitchen torch, toast the marshmallow (do this just before serving).

3 Serve immediately.

Note You'll have leftover Marshmallow Topping, to which you can add a bit of crispy cereal and set on the counter for a few hours to turn into a crunchy cereal treat. Alternatively, spoon it over some hot coffee or cocoa to drink while you finish cooking.

Champagne and Strawberries

MAKES FIVE 3 TO 4 OUNCE (88 TO 118 ML) SEMISPHERICAL MOLDS OR ONE 1-QUART (1 L) MOLD

This is an absolutely glorious gelatin presentation. It would be a beautiful addition at any bridal luncheon, baby shower, or even a wedding reception. If you're making it in a large mold, just remember to grease it before adding the gelatin.

- 5 sheets gelatin, broken into pieces
- 2 cups (473 ml) champagne or prosecco
- 3 tablespoons (36 g) superfine sugar
- Juice of ½ lemon, well strained of any pulp
- 25 sheets edible gold leaf
- 5 large strawberries, stemmed

Make the Champagne Gelatin

1 Place the gelatin pieces into a heatproof bowl. Add just enough champagne to cover and set aside to bloom for 10 minutes. Place the remaining champagne in a medium bowl and set aside.

2 Set up a double boiler and an ice-water bath (see box, page 127); set the ice-water bath aside.

3 Place the heatproof bowl of gelatin onto the double boiler, making sure that the bottom of the bowl does not touch the water. Heat, stirring occasionally, until the gelatin has completely dissolved, about 3 minutes. Add the sugar and heat, stirring gently and constantly, until the sugar has dissolved, about another 3 minutes. Stir in the lemon juice and remove the bowl from the saucepan.

4 Place a fine-mesh sieve over the bowl of remaining champagne and pour the hot gelatin mixture through it. Remove the sieve and stir to blend completely.

(continued)

Add the Gold Leaf

1 Place the bowl of champagne gelatin into the ice-water bath and, stirring constantly, add the gold leaf. Continue stirring until the gelatin begins to set and the gold leaf is suspended throughout, about 5 minutes.

2 Pour about 1 tablespoon of the champagne gelatin into each of the molds. Transfer to the freezer to chill until completely set, about 15 minutes.

Insert the Strawberries

1 Gently place 4 toothpicks equidistant around the stem end of each strawberry. Remove the molds from the freezer and suspend a strawberry, tip downward, into each, taking care that the stem end is even with the top of the mold. Return the molds to the freezer and let set until quite firm, about 15 minutes.

2 Remove the molds from the freezer and carefully remove and discard the toothpicks. Fill each mold to the top with the remaining champagne gelatin. Refrigerate until completely set, at least 2 hours or up to 8 hours.

Unmold It

1 When ready to serve, remove the molds from the refrigerator. Working with one at time, gently push on the silicone and the gelatin should pop right out into your hand. Quickly transfer the champagne dome, rounded side up, onto a dessert plate.

2 Serve immediately.

Boozy Birch Beer Float

MAKES 12 COUPE GLASSES

This recipe is inspired by one of my favorite childhood desserts, a birch beer float. Growing up in Philadelphia, we always had a bottle of Pennsylvania Dutch Birch Beer in the fridge. On special nights, my mom would make us all floats using the sweet and bubbly drink topped off with a scoop of vanilla ice cream.

I included a little bourbon in this grown-up version. If you are not a fan of bourbon, vanilla vodka is a great alternative. A bit of edible glitter will really wow your guests.

BIRCH BEER GELATIN

6 cups (1.4 L) birch beer or root beer

6 teaspoons (three 7 g packets) unflavored gelatin powder, such as Knox brand (see Note)

½ cup (118 ml) bourbon or vanilla vodka

½ cup (100 g) sugar

1 teaspoon edible white pearlescent glitter

VANILLA CREAM GELATIN

1 quart (1 L) heavy cream

1 vanilla bean, split lengthwise, seeds scraped

½ cup (100 g) sugar

3 tablespoons (45 ml) water

1 packet (7 g) unflavored gelatin powder, such as Knox brand

Make the Birch Beer Gelatin

1 Place 1 cup (237 ml) of the birch beer in a medium saucepan. Sprinkle the gelatin over the top and set aside to bloom for 10 minutes.

2 Add the remaining 5 cups (1.2 L) of birch beer and place over medium heat. Cook, stirring constantly, until the gelatin has dissolved completely, about 5 minutes. Stir in the bourbon and sugar and continue to heat until the sugar has dissolved. Add the glitter and remove from the heat. Refrigerate until the mixture begins to thicken, stirring occasionally to distribute the glitter, about 30 minutes.

3 Remove from the refrigerator and spoon an equal portion of the birch beer gelatin into each of twelve coupe glasses, filling the glasses about three-fourths full. Place the glasses in the refrigerator and chill until completely set, about 1 hour.

Make the Vanilla Cream Gelatin

1 Place the cream, vanilla bean and seeds, and sugar in a medium saucepan over medium heat. Bring to a simmer, then immediately remove the saucepan from the heat. Cover and set aside to infuse the cream with the vanilla, about 15 minutes.

2 Place the water in a small bowl. Sprinkle the gelatin over the top and set aside to bloom for 10 minutes.

3 Uncover the cream mixture and return to medium heat. Bring to a simmer; then immediately remove from the heat. Add the gelatin mixture and stir until the gelatin has dissolved completely, about 4 minutes. Let cool to room temperature (it must not be warm).

Build the Layers

1 Remove the glasses from the refrigerator. Divide the cream mixture over the top of the set birch beer layer. Cover each glass with plastic film and refrigerate until completely set, about 6 hours or no more than 24 hours.

2 When ready to serve, remove the glasses from the refrigerator. Unwrap and serve immediately.

Note Each 7-gram packet of Knox Unflavored Gelatine will yield about 2½ teaspoons of powder. For this recipe you will need 4 packets total.

Bloody Mary Brunch Shot

MAKES 10 SHOTS

This is a zesty way to begin a brunch! And to end one, too!!! Laughs come easily as guests try to pop the shot into their mouths in one big gulp while also managing the shrimp. Without the added gelatin, this recipe can be easily doubled or tripled to make the very tasty classic cocktail.

½ cup (118 ml) tomato juice

2 tablespoons fresh lemon juice

1 packet (7 g) unflavored gelatin powder, such as Knox brand

½ cup (118 ml) vodka

1 teaspoon prepared horseradish

1 teaspoon Worcestershire sauce

Coarse salt and freshly ground black pepper

10 cooked shrimp, tails on, peeled and deveined for garnish

1 tablespoon finely chopped fresh dill for garnish (optional)

1 Combine the tomato and lemon juices in a small saucepan over medium heat. Bring to a bare simmer. Immediately add the gelatin and whisk vigorously to combine.

2 Remove from the heat and whisk in the vodka, horseradish, and Worcestershire sauce. Season with salt and pepper. Set aside to cool.

3 Divide the cooled tomato mixture equally among ten shot glasses and let them set in the refrigerator for 15 to 20 minutes until the mixture starts to thicken slightly. Remove the glasses from the refrigerator and carefully curl a shrimp over the edge of each glass and return to the refrigerator until the gelatin is completely set, about 2 hours.

4 About 15 minutes before ready to serve, remove the shots from the refrigerator. Allow to sit until the edges of the gelatin begin to pull away from the glass very slightly (this makes the shots easier to consume in one gulp). Sprinkle them with dill, if desired, before serving.

Shootin' the Breeze

MAKES 2 CUPS (473 ML) OR 16 SHOTS

This is my idea of a perfect beach gelatin shot. The combination of pineapple and cranberry is just so refreshing. You can use vodka or coconut rum for these; whichever you choose, just make sure to include it in both layers. Although I always serve gelatin shots when they are completely set, you can also remove them from the refrigerator about 45 minutes before serving so that they are easier to "drink" as the gelatin pulls away from the glass.

PINEAPPLE GELATIN

¾ cup (177 ml) pineapple juice

1¼ teaspoons unflavored gelatin powder, such as Knox brand

¼ cup (59 ml) vodka or Malibu Coconut Rum

Juice of 1 lime

CRANBERRY GELATIN

¾ cup (177 ml) cranberry juice cocktail

1¼ teaspoons unflavored gelatin powder, such as Knox brand

¼ cup (59 ml) vodka or Malibu Coconut Rum

¼ teaspoon edible pink glitter

Make the Pineapple Gelatin

1 Place the pineapple juice in a small saucepan. Sprinkle the gelatin over the top and set aside to bloom for 10 minutes.

2 Place the pineapple gelatin mixture in the saucepan over low heat and cook, stirring constantly, until the gelatin has dissolved, about 4 minutes. Remove from the heat and stir in the vodka and lime juice. Pour the mixture through a fine-mesh sieve into a small bowl. Let cool to room temperature.

3 Divide the pineapple mixture among sixteen shot glasses. It should come about halfway up. Transfer to the freezer to chill until completely set, about 30 minutes.

Make the Cranberry Gelatin

1 Place the cranberry juice cocktail in a small saucepan. Sprinkle the gelatin over the top and set aside to bloom for 10 minutes.

2 Place the saucepan over low heat and cook, stirring constantly, until the gelatin has dissolved, about 4 minutes. Remove from the heat and stir in the vodka. Pour the mixture through a fine-mesh sieve into a small bowl. Transfer to the freezer to chill until thickened, about 30 minutes.

Build the Layers

1 Remove the bowl from the freezer and gently stir in the glitter to suspend it throughout; do not overmix.

2 Spoon an equal portion of the cranberry gelatin over the pineapple gelatin in each of the shot glasses. Refrigerate until completely set, about 2 hours. Serve in the shot glasses.

Watermelon Margarita Bites

MAKES 2 CUPS (473 ML) OR 16 SHOTS

This gelatin shot is a juicy, summery take on a margarita and perfect for a hot day. Fresh watermelon juice is so refreshing and light, which makes it very easy to enjoy more than one.

1¾ cups (415 ml) watermelon juice

1 packet (7 g) unflavored gelatin powder, such as Knox brand

Juice of 2 limes

¼ cup (59 ml) blanco tequila

2 tablespoons Cointreau

¼ cup (50 g) sugar

⅛ teaspoon edible rose gold glitter

Black sea salt for garnish (optional)

16 small lime wedges for garnish (optional)

1 Place the watermelon juice in a small saucepan. Sprinkle the gelatin over the top and set aside to bloom for 10 minutes.

2 Add the lime juice, tequila, Cointreau, and sugar and place over low heat. Cook, stirring constantly, until the sugar has dissolved, about 4 minutes. Pour the mixture through a fine-mesh sieve into a small bowl. Refrigerate until the mixture has thickened somewhat, about 30 minutes.

3 Remove the bowl from the refrigerator and gently stir in the glitter until it is suspended throughout; do not overmix. Spoon an equal portion of the watermelon mixture into each of sixteen shot glasses. The shots can be stored in the refrigerator for up to 6 hours.

4 When ready to serve, garnish each shot with a sprinkle of black sea salt and a lime wedge and serve immediately.

Holiday Spiced Mulled Wine

MAKES ONE 6-CUP (1.4 L) MOLD

When unmolded onto a large platter garnished with fresh fruit, such as grapes, lady apples, tiny pears, and some greenery, this gelatin can serve as the centerpiece on a holiday buffet table. It is a stunning presentation and tastes so good, too. If you are not a fan of alcohol, you can replace the wine with any cranberry juice mix.

Vegetable oil for greasing the mold

2 large organic navel oranges

3¼ cups (769 ml) Chianti Classico or other rich Italian red wine

1¼ cups (296 ml) brandy

1 cup (237 ml) cranberry juice cocktail

½ cup (107 g) dark brown sugar

2 cinnamon sticks

6 whole cloves

2 star anise

1 vanilla bean, split lengthwise

4 packets (7 g each) unflavored gelatin powder, such as Knox brand

2 firm apples, peeled, cored, and diced

2 pears, peeled, cored, and diced

Prep the Mold

Lightly grease the interior of a 6-cup (1.4 L) mold with vegetable oil. Set aside.

Make the Spiced Wine Gelatin

1 Using a vegetable peeler, carefully remove fine strips of zest from one of the oranges (avoid any pith) and set aside. Juice the orange and set the juice aside. Using a sharp knife, trim off each end of the remaining orange. Then, cut the orange, crosswise, into slices about ¼ inch (0.64 cm) thick. Set aside.

(continued)

2 Combine the orange juice with the peel in a large saucepan. Add the red wine, brandy, cranberry juice cocktail, brown sugar, cinnamon sticks, cloves, star anise, and vanilla bean and place over medium heat. Cook, stirring constantly, until the sugar dissolves, about 3 minutes. Increase the heat to high and bring to a boil. Immediately reduce the heat to low and continue to cook at a gentle simmer until the flavors have blended completely, about 30 minutes.

3 Remove the spiced wine mixture from the heat and pour the mixture through a fine-mesh sieve into a clean bowl, discarding the solids. Place 1 cup (237 ml) of the spiced wine into a large saucepan (reserve the rest). Sprinkle the gelatin over the top and set aside to bloom for 10 minutes.

4 Add the reserved spiced wine to the gelatin mixture and place the saucepan over low heat. Cook, stirring constantly, until the gelatin melts, about 5 minutes. Remove from the heat and again pour the mixture through a fine-mesh sieve into a clean medium bowl. Refrigerate, stirring occasionally, until beginning to thicken, about 1 hour.

Add the Fruit

1 Remove the gelatin from the refrigerator, stir in the apples and pears, then spoon the gelatin into the prepared mold.

2 Wrap the entire mold in plastic film and return to the refrigerator and let set for at least 4 hours or up to 24 hours.

Unmold It

1 Remove the mold from the refrigerator. Remove and discard the plastic film. Place the mold in a large bowl of hot water for about 15 seconds to loosen, taking care that the water does not come up over the edge of the mold. Watch carefully as you do not want the gelatin to begin melting. Remove the mold from the water and wipe the exterior dry.

2 Place a serving plate over the mold and invert the mold onto it. The gelatin should pop right out. Serve immediately.

Sources

Black cherry syrup:
Filthy Food; filthyfood.com; 786-916-5556

Candied walnuts and orange peel:
Nuts.com; 800-558-6887

Cotton candy:
Rainbow Cotton Candy; rainbowcottoncandy.com; 800-726-8918

Cotton candy flavor:
LorAnn Oils; lorannoils.com; 800-862-8620

Decorative sprinkles, edible glitter:
Foliay; foliay.com; info@foliay.com

D&G Genuine Jamaican Cream Soda:
Amazon.com

Sheet gelatin, sprinkles, flavorings:
Confectionery House; confectioneryhouse.com; 518-279-3179

Silicone molds:
Pastry Chef Central; pastrychef.com; 888-750-CHEF

Acknowledgments

This book would not have been possible without the love and support of so many people around me. From the very early days of my exploration into the wonderfully wiggly world of gelatin, my good friend and coauthor Judith Choate has been an endless source of encouragement and knowledge. This book would never have happened without her.

Thanks to the Stevens family for always being the most gracious guinea pigs; Guto Barra for allowing me the time and space to tackle this project; Ryan Gialames, Kelly Potchak, and Maria Gismondi (BCDC) for being the most incredible cheerleaders and friends; Camille Rodriquez for her culinary wisdom; and Steve Pool for being a creative force in my life.

I also have to give a huge thank-you to my family for always encouraging me to explore my creativity, and to my husband, Raymond Moore, for not only patiently dealing with a small New York City kitchen full of random gelatin molds, but also the late nights and a seemingly endless parade of samples forced upon him.

—Peter DiMario

Index

Note: Page references in *italics* indicate recipe photographs.

D

E

M

N

O

P

R

About the Authors

Peter DiMario is a New York–based multiple NY Emmy Award–winning producer/writer for film and television. Peter brings with him his background in art, psychology, and design along with a deep love of all things theater. Born and raised in Philadelphia in a food-loving Italian American family, his passion for culinary arts can be credited to his great-grandmother and his grandmother who never seemed to leave the kitchen.

Judith Choate is a recipe developer, writer, and chef who has contributed to more than 100 cookbooks including three James Beard Award–winning cookbooks, one of which also won a Julia Child IACP Award.